DAGGETT

CREATING THE NORTH AMERICAN LANDSCAPE
Gregory Conniff, Bonnie Loyd, Edward K. Muller,
and David Schuyler, *Consulting Editors*
Published in cooperation with the Center for American Places,
Harrisonburg, Virginia

DAGGETT

Life in a Mojave Frontier Town

DIX VAN DYKE

Edited by Peter Wild

THE JOHNS HOPKINS UNIVERSITY PRESS
Baltimore & London

© 1997 The Johns Hopkins University Press
All rights reserved. Published 1997
Printed in the United States of America on acid-free paper
06 05 04 03 02 01 00 99 98 97   5 4 3 2 1

The Johns Hopkins University Press
2715 North Charles Street
Baltimore, Maryland 21218-4319
The Johns Hopkins Press Ltd., London

Library of Congress Cataloging-in-Publication Data will be found
at the end of this book.
A catalog record for this book is available from the British Library.

ISBN 0-8018-5625-6

Contents

Illustrations

Following page 84

Acknowledgments

So many people gave of their time and knowledge in helping with this project that I would need pages to thank them appropriately. Barring that, I list some of their names: Clifford Walker, Beryl Bell, Gordon and Donna Stricler, Sally West, Eugene Stoops, Ronald H. Limbaugh, Me Linda Johnson, Michael E. Hamblin, Lois Olsrud, James H. Maguire, Donald A. Barclay, Roger Myers, Peter Steere, Lawrence Alf, Neil Carmony, William Kleese, Jack and Marjorie Van Dyke, Marcia Marma, Merrill McCarty, Virginia R. Harshman, Arda Haenszel, Peggy Flyntz, Thom Thompson, Larry Stephenson, Robert Walker, Scott Borden, Robert Williams, Lucile Weight, Dennis G. Casebier, and Margot Spangenberg. Over the years, Germaine L. Moon has been particularly helpful in supplying information. Dix's nephew, Alan Golden, shared his time and knowledge as we tramped across the Van Dyke Ranch, where he was born.

The grace of my research assistant, Laura Howard, knew no bounds, even when it came to leaping the Mojave River on a cold day.

I particularly thank George F. Thompson, president of the Center for American Places, for his enthusiasm and good guidance.

I thank the Mojave River Valley Museum for permission to print large portions of the Dix manuscript in its holdings, and I thank the *Desert Dispatch*, descendant of the *Barstow Printer Review*, for permission to use much of the Dix material that appeared in the newspaper's pages after Dix's death.

DAGGETT

INTRODUCTION

OFF IN EUROPE, Cézanne was working out the spatial problems of his famous *Bathers,* while in the United States an anarchist shocked the nation by shooting President McKinley. Such events, however, hardly caused a riffle in Daggett, a little boom town lost out in the Mojave Desert and addicted to its own excitements. The town would not long enjoy the luxury of its splendid isolation. Told by a local rancher, the following is the story of how the twentieth century arrived in a wild frontier town and tamed it into modern times. But first, meet some of its characters.

Meet Fat Etta, China Mary, and Mother Preston. The last, a madam of sumptuous proportions and valorous spirit, was wont to lock the head of an unruly client in the crook of an immense arm. Then, as he twisted hopelessly in her human vise, she proceeded to beat his face with her windmilling fist.

Meet the Prophet Elijah, who communed with Celestial Visitors.

Or, if you're up to it, introduce yourself to any number of leftovers from the hard school of the frontier. Living, Dix tells us, "on wild game and mesquite beans," they lived in crude cabins down in the riverbottom. Feeling crowded by changing conditions, they were likely to greet intruders with drawn guns. Not characters to meet if you're out for a stroll, inadvertently trespassing on their wild domain. And, in contrast, the judge with the rasping voice. He left such local types pretty much alone to work out their own frontier dynamics, while offering feasts of watermelon and kindly advice to the downtrodden.

And meet the town, too. One night when gunplay broke out in the crowded Bucket of Blood Saloon and the smoke cleared, revealing a body on the floor, there were no witnesses to the heinous crime. That was typical. With characteristic sangfroid, the verdict of the pickup

I

jury was "death by parties unknown." Then, after the pesky interruption, the good citizens of boom-town Daggett trooped back to their saloons and dreams of fabulous silver deposits in the hills.

Or, far from town, we watch a cowboy sleeping out on the range scramble to his knees and with clutched pistol confront a banshee moaning toward him out of the desert blackness.

Western literature has plenty of diaries and reminiscences by old-timers. Most of them offer, beyond amusing misspellings and bad grammar, such fare as "Rode ten miles today. Found the waterhole dry. Weather hot." Fare that gets old fast. In other words, most of them are boring. Though they doggedly record personal events and may be of a certain historical value, they are trapped in the repetitive and the mundane. This is because the authors rarely develop their larger context, the complex world beyond themselves, and rarely do such writers have an artist's eye for those details that bring color to the cheeks of daily events for those of us in far more docile times.

In contrast and to our pleasure, we watch frontier Daggett swirl, quickened before us in the following pages. To our good fortune, Dix Van Dyke's writing about his wild town far out in Southern California's desert is both lively and authentic.

Yet there's a danger here. In opposing the Disney Company's plans to turn a site near the Manassas Battlefield in Virginia into a theme park, Civil War historian and novelist Shelby Foote warned about what he called "attractive distortions." That is, the danger, for the sake of keeping the turnstiles spinning, of emphasizing those immediately exciting features of the past at the expense of the far more complex aspects lying behind them. For most of us, brought up on largely fake Hollywood images of the Wild West dancing in our heads, this is a very real danger, indeed, when it comes to Dix. We long for what we want to see—the brothels, shootouts, and herds of stampeding cattle. These are the familiar candies most of us were fed about the West, and here they certainly reward with quick excitements.

Almost as if he were anticipating this, Dix warns that, for most of the time, life in Daggett was boring. Yes, Saturday nights could get lively in the saloons, and there were times when the able-bodied men of the town dropped whatever they were doing and, grabbing rifles loaded with real bullets, rode off into the real adrenaline rush of pursuing a murderer across the desert. But for the most part, even in the midst of its boom-town heydays, when silver was pouring out of the nearby hills and fortunes were made and lost overnight on the streets of Daggett, the townspeople worked in their stores, labored in their fields, and the children went to school. Like people everywhere, Daggett's citizens regularly put their shoulders to the rather unexciting business of getting through another day.

In such a milieu, when Frank and Homer Ryerse's general store burned to the ground one night in 1908, it was a grand and memorable event. Tumbling out of bed with excitement, "everyone . . . attended" and watched the great conflagration, says Dix. Even today, generations later, it remains a landmark date stuck in the memory of a town that doesn't easily forget.

In reflecting Daggett's rhythms, Dix did not write a mostly boring book occasionally relieved with the nuggets of chromatic events. Though uneducated, Dix was the self-appointed local historian of the area, and he was a natural for the job. Where most other recorders of the frontier failed, he perceived the nuances both in large events and in everyday tasks. Though he certainly recounts here the struggles and woes of trying to grow crops on the desert, he does so as part of a larger picture. His mind ranges beyond his own immediate concerns to capture the economic, sociological, geographical, and psychological forces—as well as the personal conflicts and dramas—at work as his little town evolves from the frontier into the twentieth century. Beyond an eye for humor, even humor mocking his own occasional gaffes, he has the novelist's eye for catching just the right details, which bring the characters striding through his pages into sharp and memorable focus. Lastly, strange to most of us in our crowded lives, in a vast, new land, a frontier with few people, each person takes on an individuality of near iconographic importance, as if each were a character in a Noh play, and Dix catches this unique quality, too.

Dix's account, however, has advantages beyond its writer's native talent and the immediacy of barroom bang-bang. Simply put, Daggett was an interesting place.

As outsiders still find to their amazement as they drive across Southern California, the Mojave is an immense desert. As the hours go by and the tires hum, the barren mountain ranges and sandy sweeps stretch endlessly between the Arizona border and the lush, snow-topped coastal range. Occasionally, to left and right off the highway appear vast lakes, but they are lakes of sand, perhaps shimmering with mirages of water but holding the real thing only rarely, when snowmelt from mountains many miles away roars down the desert's normally dry watercourses. In frontier times, this was an even more forbidding, and downright dangerous, place. Its wagon-bogging sands, rampaging Indians, and waterless distances created a noxious barrier to the palmy Pacific shore waiting ahead. On top of that, the Mojave was viciously hot. No wonder people enduring the weeks it took to cross this broad desert sneered at it as God's Mistake and cursed the place as the Devil's Domain.

Then, in 1881, two prospectors struck a rich vein of silver in the Calico Mountains. From here poured millions and millions of dollars of silver—the richest discovery of silver in Southern California's history. This, together with local borax mines, created Daggett. Located out on the desert flats six miles from the silver strike, the town had important railroad connections and a crucial, if elusive, water supply from the nearby Mojave River. Because of these advantages, Daggett became a busy supply point for the Calicos. As the frenzy for riches increased and other mines mushroomed across the desert, Daggett's teamsters soon were hauling heavy equipment and the all-important whiskey over vast distances. As Dix shows, this was bitter, grueling work. The mines in the natural furnace of Death Valley, for instance, lay about 130 miles north of Daggett. Those were hideous miles for man and beast slogging day after day under a punishing sun through sand and over bare and waterless mountains.

At the other extreme, the free-flowing money, fantastic dreams of even greater riches, and the wild isolation of the desert also made Daggett a place of brothels and saloons, of gamblers and bizarre misfits. Out there in the desert, they could play out their freewheeling lives, brutal as they could be, with little concern for the law and the other restraints of far-off civilization. Distant cities such as San Bernardino and Los Angeles, developing the accoutrements of sedate society such as libraries and women's clubs, heard the stories filtering back across the desert and scowled at churchless Daggett. To them it was a lurid and barbarous hotbed of vice. Indeed, according to one authority, no one in Daggett ever went to heaven.

Which is to say that Dix had good material to write about. And much to his credit, Dix had the wisdom to see such people not as brightly painted cardboard figures moving across the stage of his frontier but as individuals often in conflict with their fellows—and, furthermore, with their changing times.

In Stephen Crane's whimsical "The Bride Comes to Yellow Sky," published in 1898, we see a western town still dreaming of its frontier days even as civilization overwhelms its sustaining fantasies. In 1901, Dix arrived in a Daggett at roughly the same stage of development as the Yellow Sky in Crane's short story. That is, Dix arrived at a point of conflicting change, and with considerable humor and pathos he paints Daggett as it moves, kicking rather vigorously, from the robust frontier into more staid modern times. Beyond its ready entertainment value, this is perhaps Dix's chief contribution. When we readers see the notorious Bucket of Blood Saloon begin to sell ice cream and soda pop, we shudder, knowing deep in our bones that an era has passed, never to return.

Dix's story has much more going for it beyond that—or, to give him proper credit, Dix has the acumen to use the advantages innate in his material. The Van Dyke Ranch became something of an unlikely crossroads for intellectually bright people, some of them famous. Here Dix shows us aging Sierra explorer and conservationist John Muir visiting the ranch, then taking sick with his final illness while at his daughter's nearby house. Admirers of Muir may well be surprised at the tangle of family relations begun when daughter Helen marries Buel Funk, whose father was a partner at the ranch. It's a story never told before in print.*

Also as to personages at the ranch, Dix's uncle John C. Van Dyke put in periodic appearances. A refined critic and a professor of art at well-known Rutgers University in New Brunswick, New Jersey, Uncle Jack was the author of *The Desert*. This was the first, and is still the most famous, book written in praise of America's arid lands. Perhaps out of a certain family loyalty, Dix doesn't comment on his uncle's book. Lovely as the volume is, it also stands as one of the great put-ons in western American literature.† Dix does work in, however, a couple of wry, left-handed digs at his famed uncle, and—literary historians take note—Dix shows the paths of Uncle Jack and John Muir fatefully crossing at the ranch and the two writers going at each other hammer and tongs.

All of which is to say that Dix tells a number of parallel stories here—of barroom brawls and brothels, of mining claims, ghosts, cattle drives, and suicides. He shows the delicate beauty of the desert and the human hopes that often ended in folly there, and he doesn't avoid the intricacies of his relationship with his renowned but sometimes cranky father. All this Dix weaves synchronously into a colorful pattern telling not only of Daggett but of all humankind.

Dix's several tales contain yet another strong ingredient. It is the personal story of how two men sweated through the years, battling

---

*Expanding on the context of what Dix says, I have followed John Muir to the ranch in "John Muir and the Desert Connection" and "John Muir and the Van Dyke Ranch," parts 1 and 2.

†John C. Van Dyke's *The Desert* appeared in 1901, the same year that Dix and his father, Theodore, moved permanently to Daggett. However, Theodore's familiarity with the desert went back long before that (see Dix Van Dyke to Alice [Salisbury], 22 Dec. 1949). Wild and Carmony suggest that urbanite John C. Van Dyke obtained much of the material for his imagined desert heroics during trips to Southern California, where he pumped brother Theodore and other locals for information. In fact, Dix provided some desert notes for a 1930 edition of *The Desert*, and although Dix emends and modifies some statements in the text, he does so gently, and is not nearly the critic of his uncle's skewed facts that he might have been.

drought and rabbits and searing winds in hopes of making their desert ranch prosper—and battling along the way their litigious partners determined to evict the Van Dykes from the homestead they held dear.

And lurking behind this is another story still.

Dix opens with a masterly scene. Rivaling the bleakness of a Bergman film, Dix shows us a sick old man and his son driving their wagon into Daggett, a town so blighted the few surviving trees seem to be "abandoning the struggle for existence." Immediately we wonder why the two outsiders have thrown their lot with such an unpromising prospect. What would push dignified Theodore Strong Van Dyke, scion of a wealthy, aristocratic family and a well-known writer in his own right, far out beyond the world of servants and tinkling crystal that was his heritage into a forlorn desert burg of crude manners and crumbling false-front adobes to start a new life? Together with son Dix, an unschooled misfit, they must have made a strange couple in frontier Daggett—though not so strange, considering the society of outcasts into which they were plunging.

It is a story Dix keeps touching on but never tells completely, perhaps because of the pain it caused him. And though many of the details may never be known, it is a story we need to piece together at least briefly here, not only as background for these unique chronicles of a boom town, but also as a broader story of disappointments and bright hopes that is the lot of us all.

Theodore Strong Van Dyke was born in 1842 at Green Oaks, an august three-peaked mansion in the idyllic countryside of rolling fields and woods surrounding New Brunswick, New Jersey. Since 1652, when Thomasse Janse Van Dyke arrived in New Amsterdam from the Netherlands, the Van Dykes and the families into which they married had taken their place as part of the nation's powerful, though unofficial, aristocracy. The line included Revolutionary War heroes, a renowned mathematician, a famous spy, a famous poet, and a host of civic leaders.[*]

John, Theodore's father, was by turns a lawyer, bank president,

---

[*] *The Raritan,* by John C. Van Dyke, surveys the family's history.

congressman, and member of New Jersey's supreme court. A deft politician, he played a large role in the maneuvers that eventually made Abraham Lincoln president. Yet all did not go well for John. In old age—family rumor attributes it to political setbacks—John uprooted his family and moved them to the wilds of Minnesota. There he built another mansion, this time a three-story affair high on a bluff overlooking the broad Mississippi River. Ten years later, in 1878, he died. Though a prosperous man, he was gnawed by disappointments. According to John C. Van Dyke, Theodore's brother, "nervous morbidity" and "bleak pessimism" ran through the family in counterbalance to the ambition and buoyant spirits driving individual members to success (*The Raritan*, 87). The warring traits go some distance in explaining the irony and heady romance combined in a set of tensions often brightening the writing of the Van Dykes.

In the meantime, Theodore graduated from Princeton University and was admitted to the bar. During the Minnesota period, he married, practiced law, and served in the state legislature. Yet bad health—probably tuberculosis—plagued him, and in 1875 he abandoned gelid Minnesota for the warmth of Southern California. He lived first in San Diego, then in Los Angeles, but, always an enthusiastic outdoorsman, he spent much of his time tramping through the surrounding mountains and deserts, hunting, exploring, and in the process regaining his health in Southern California's balmy climate.

He also turned this enjoyable regimen into a livelihood. Ranging far into Mexico with rifle, dog, and horse, he became one of the foremost and most authoritative outdoors writers of the day. He not only earned a living producing articles for the nation's major magazines and newspapers. Among his many works is *Game Birds at Home,* a graciously knowledgeable book of rambles. In 1902, Theodore showed his solid connections when he collaborated with naturalist President Theodore Roosevelt and others to produce *The Deer Family.* Van Dyke's main literary accomplishments, however, are two wry novels, *Millionaires of a Day* and the mildly risqué and entertaining *Flirtation Camp.*

In the process, understandably so, given the climate that had pulled him back from the grave, Theodore became a booster of his adopted land. But he was a booster of a different sort. In contrast to the hucksters fleecing the public with scams during the real-estate fever of the 1880s, Theodore's *Millionaires of a Day* warned that true progress would come from more than making "money out of wind" (92). Farsighted and astute, Theodore had a Virgilian vision of the future, one in which man would work with, rather than against, nature to produce a lasting prosperity (Wyatt, 149).

In the mid-1880s, as part of this vision, Theodore joined with a number of other civic leaders to found the San Diego Flume Company. For its day a radical plan of grand proportions, this was an unprecedented scheme to bring water gushing through pipes and over trestles down out of the mountains and into seaside San Diego. Somewhat to the public's amazement, the elaborate project eventually worked, assuring San Diego's transition from a sleepy coastal village into a dynamic city. In addition to his writing reputation, Theodore now wore the mantle of a hydraulic engineer who could do wonders.

Those were heady days, when gold, water, and silver were pouring out of the hills. If such marvels of prosperity were happening, what further miracles of riches lay in the future? Even the wastelands of the desert might be turned into agricultural wonderlands. When, as Dix tells us, a water-development company ran into trouble with its project out in the Mojave Desert, the backers naturally enough turned to Theodore, and he naturally enough accepted. Or so it seems.

According to the promotional brochure *Minneola Valley*, it is true that by the mid-1890s, Theodore was dabbling in desert water investments. Could it be that, along with many another solid businessman on the Coast, he, too, became dazzled and was swept away by the optimistic tide of fantasies that often ended in their backers' financial loss? If there is truth in this, it certainly isn't the whole story. A good deal of evidence suggests that much more lay behind Theodore's radical move to Daggett than a temporary fling with desert follies.

Practically everything in Theodore's long years in California points to caution, reason, and circumspection when it came to land development. Analyzing the various soils of Southern California, its climate, and economic prospects, his *Southern California* rationally laid out the pros and cons of settling in the region, and he wrote an entire novel, the aforementioned *Millionaires of a Day,* burlesquing the willful ignorance that led investors lemminglike into the mass financial ruin of the 1880s land boom. True, he had broken ground with his San Diego Flume Company, but that was a reasoned, if unprecedented, adventure. After all, any shrewd businessman could tell that there *was* abundant water in the mountains behind San Diego. The problem here was a practical one, getting water down to the city, and it was a problem that forward-looking men solved.

In woeful contrast, such conditions did not obtain in the nearly waterless Mojave Desert. There, only about three to five skimpy inches of precipitation fell each year, and the Mojave River, beside which the dusty town of Daggett squatted like a stray dog panting for a drink, for most of its length was a dry streambed. Flowing northeast out of the forested San Bernardino Mountains, only to disappear in the desert sands, the intermittent river ran generous supplies of water only after gullywashers or when snowmelt from the distant peaks brought the spring floods. A few years earlier, in 1886, Theodore had himself sized up the current enthusiasm for developing the desert and concluded that "most of it cannot be irrigated at all. . . . The rainfall is generally so light and the hot winds are so common that cultivation is at present out of the question, and the desert is practically uninhabitable" (*County of San Diego,* 32). And yet, there he was.

And not only there, but also old, sick, and broke.

Bullheaded Theodore may have had hope in his heart when he moved to Daggett, but likely a set of personal crises helped push him far out into the desert, where, as Dix says, he faced "an appalling situation." Dix shows the two, father and son, badly out of their element and struggling through years of privation and bleak prospects, hanging on despite everything, as if making a home in this forlorn place were an act of desperation after all else had failed. More than likely it had. Dix's earlier manuscript, "Recollections of Boyhood Days in San Diego," hints at a domestic life rife with marital tensions. This, together with other family anomalies, is borne out by Theodore's divorce only two years before he left for the desert, and this in a time when such a rift carried a heavier stigma than it does today.* Added to that, Theodore copyrighted two of his early books, *Flirtation Camp* and *The Still-Hunter*, in the name of brother John, as if, under the copyright laws of the day, to protect the author's assets. Marital and/or financial crises contributed to driving Theodore out into the desert. In this he followed the pattern of his own father, who, when about Theodore's same age and suffering setbacks in New Jersey, yanked the family up abruptly by the roots and moved it to the wilds of Minnesota.

A father worshiper, Dix is careful to protect Theodore on such disturbing matters. However, he's hardly protective of himself. Though he doesn't mention that he had a defective right eye and a speech impediment, he frankly admits that he, too, was an outcast, though in ways rather different from his father's. Uneducated, a young man in his early twenties when his lifelong stay in Daggett begins, he's been unable to gain his sea legs in proper society. Instead, he's wandered about as a hobo, the familiar of "jungle buzzards, bundle stiffs . . . gay cats, and the flotsam and jetsam" that rides the rails. In fact, at times Dix seems proud of his derelict proclivities and stiff-backed individualism—proud that he reads books at night when the other hands are playing cards, proud that he doesn't give a tinker's dam for the diversions money can buy, except for an occasional nickel cigar. When neighbors try to find him a wife, he laughs at their folly. When later in life he travels to Catalina Island for a rare holiday, he flees in horror from the crowds of tourists. Instead, he finds peace up in the wild mountains with the kindly, unsophisticated mountain folk.

All in all, what emerges is the portrait of a wry, somewhat eccentric, but avuncular man with a twinkle in his one good eye—a good guide for our tour of Daggett.

---

*See Divorce Decree of Theodore Van Dyke. Unfortunately, the details of the divorce are somewhat clouded because of a missing file.

Though Hollywood's images of western characters often are exaggerated and simplified, it does appear that the frontier had more than its share of individuals whose personalities broke the bounds of what we think of as the norm. Stories about Dix's friend Death Valley Scotty, a mercurial and elusive desert rat who claimed to own a secret gold mine, grew to such proportions that one tale has him appearing in the streets of San Bernardino, hilariously throwing money from his wagon as he passed through the city. The truth is bizarre enough. Enjoying access to funds given him by an eccentric millionaire, Scotty built a castle in Death Valley and once chartered a train to take him from Los Angeles to Chicago. On a less happy note is Bill Frakes, the anger inside him on hair trigger as he prowled about looking for an excuse to whip someone at gunpoint. According to the way Dix presents him, today he most likely would be locked up as a criminal.

Did the frontier attract such people, or did its relatively lax societal taboos allow the eccentricities latent even in "normal" people to bloom? Though it's a question that can be debated endlessly, the answer probably involves some of both. A few things, in any case, need to be said on this score. The frontier rarely was freewheeling for long; that is, a chaos where conflicting brute strength provided the only rule. Though the sparse population allowed wide latitude for behavior in certain respects, law and custom also set limits in others.

When the people of Daggett came together to dance, crude as they could be, social pressures kept the peace. One can imagine that the likes of Bill Frakes didn't attend. As for the others, they might drink but not get drunk. If they did and became a nuisance, Dix tells us, "their friends would lead them away." As for what was considered then the members of the weaker sex, they probably were far safer and more respected in Daggett than women in modern society. Surely their roles were more narrowly defined, but in return they benefited from the courtesy and deference conspicuously rare in many relationships today.

Despite the frontier's social amenities, both Theodore and Dix were outsiders. Small frontier towns, populated mostly by miners, saloonkeepers, prostitutes, cowboys, and a shifting population of transients, selected for certain types, and that selection process did not often include someone of Theodore's wealthy heritage, literary refinement, and education. No doubt, given his dignity, restraint, and background, something of the aristocrat's mantle clung to Theodore, qualities that could have easily worked against him—and by extension, against his son—had either shown signs of being "uppity" with the less mannered townsfolk.

Though obviously different from Daggett's general population, Theodore had the common sense or good human grace not to put on toplofty airs with his neighbors. They in turn accepted him and his son. Evidence of this is Theodore's election in 1902, soon after his arrival and by a wide margin, to be the area's justice of the peace.* The town not only elected him; it kept sending him back to office until his death in 1923.

In frontier Daggett, this was an important and prestigious office, bringing with it the title "Judge." Given the thinness of law enforcement in those rough places, it also was a potentially dangerous position. As we've seen, city folks on the Coast considered the people out on the desert a barbarous lot. Living in the remote and much scorned "cow counties," they hardly were worth the protection of the law. As Dix shows, even San Bernardino, Daggett's distant county seat, shared in the disdain. When desert ranchers contacted the district attorney about an outlaw terrorizing his neighbors, the official wrote back and mocked: "Don't you people know how to get rid of that fellow?"

Soon after, he was found dead, riddled with buckshot.

In such an atmosphere, in which far into the twentieth century good citizens and thugs alike often went about armed, vengeance could take its own course, and a man in Theodore's position ran the risk of ambush. By what accounts we have, Theodore exercised his authority wisely and without fear, coming down hard when appropriate but confident enough to bend when leniency made better sense for the community. He even was so bold as to keep the local jail at his ranch, a structure he occasionally had to guard through the night with

---

*The vote was sixty-six for Van Dyke, thirty-six for his opponent.

his shotgun when the ruffian friends of prisoners were likely to try a breakout.* And in further evidence of the community's acceptance of the Van Dykes, son Dix took over the position upon his father's death. Dix, too, was repeatedly reelected.

For loner Dix, rural Daggett was his cup of tea. Theodore may have ranted that he'd never live in a city again, but he suffered for the isolation. Whatever his love of tramping the hills with dog and gun, as a writer back in Los Angeles he'd enjoyed the company and good talk of Charles F. Lummis and other luminaries in Southern California's growing literary circle. Living far away in Daggett, and on a ranch a mile out of town, Theodore missed his former companions. Dix shows him finding some consolation in his Greek and Latin texts and all but clapping his hands when the likes of John Muir appeared at his door. Such people visiting Daggett marked rare, though treasured, moments for Theodore. All but pathetically, Dix shows his father walking to town to drink beer in search of intellectual companionship but realizing he would find none there. Despite his accomplishments and status in the community, Theodore remained a lonely man.

This hardly is a shoddy attempt at melodrama on Dix's part. His account runs the full range of genuine emotions, from the slapstick humor of barroom pranks to the deep pathos the town felt when a young woman committed suicide. In between, he can deliver the cruel facts from clinical remove—after all, he is a reporter, obliged to pass on the frontier's often brutal realities. And when a young boy, turning nimble, grabs a rifle and shoots his captor in the head, Dix can build the tensions of the drama with the skill of a playwright. Sometimes, with the frontiersman's need to survive by laughing in the midst of conflicts, he has the knack of catching both the humor and the sadness of a nasty situation. Lastly, he has a unique eye, taking delight in surreal details, as when one day he and his cowboys use fish horns to chase wild-eyed cattle.

Concerning the general time frame of *Daggett: Life in a Mojave*

---

*Historians will delight that the jail is still there at the ranch, preserved by its present owners.

Frontier Town, Dix ranges into the past to create Daggett's context. For example, he mentions the Spanish conquistadors passing through the area and brings the Anglo frontiersmen of more recent times onto his stage. His story proper, however, begins with his arrival in Daggett in 1901 and takes us through to about World War I. More significant events than the sale of ice cream and soda pop in Alex's saloon signaled the end of the frontier. One can at least guess that Dix stopped his story where he did because he realized that the onset of the automobile era heralded the triumph of technology over the old, wild days. Daggett may have sat there withering in the desert sun as a goggled Barney Oldfield tore through in his racing car for points beyond, but six miles up the road the Southern Pacific's new complex of switching yards was turning Barstow into a place of doctors and dentists, telephones and union halls—changes that did not bode well for old ways dependent on a faithful cow pony and sure aim down a rifle barrel. Dix's concluding piece involving the squabbles of the Harmony Club, taking place—of all places—in phony tepees, says as much.

In Dix's whimsical and bittersweet stories, we keep swinging from brightness to grief, though a note from a world lost always is there playing softly behind whatever tale Dix is telling. One can see this in Daggett today, its false-front buildings from frontier days still strung out along the railroad tracks, and more brightly in the good people of Daggett who retell the old stories and can show you some of the very buildings Dix mentions.

If you drive out of town a mile or so, bounce over the railroad tracks, then turn off on a bumpy road to the old Van Dyke place, you'll see a forlorn scene. Catching the eye to the left, a chimney rises boldly out of a rubble of bricks on a bleak, windblown landscape made even bleaker by Theodore's dying trees. That is the first of several ruins dotting the place. To stand there and think of Dix's feuds with the Funks and listen for the laughter of cronies Theodore and John Muir as they sit on the front porch is to feel something of the abandonment of the human heart. As few places do, the ruins of the ranch bear that flavor, bear a presence from the past—and the locals say they have seen unhappy ghosts wandering there.

One further bit of practical information might prove helpful before we turn to Dix's words themselves. The irrigation canal Dix mentions was so central to the ranchers' fortunes that it becomes almost a character—an irascible one—in these tales. Often silting up or damaged by floods, choked with weeds, and plagued by cave-ins, irrigation ditches can be pesky realities in farmers' lives, and this one was no exception. The Daggett Ditch vexed Dix with its endless demands for maintenance. To simplify Dix's discussions of it, the canal began in the Mojave River four miles upstream from the ranch, at a point where a rocky formation underground forced subterranean water to the surface. From there, the ditch ran along the south side of the river and passed through Daggett before watering the Van Dykes' fields. Despite all the troubles it caused users down through the decades, the Daggett Ditch remained in use into the 1970s, and for much of its length the course of the trench can be traced today. Water for the present fields in the area is pumped from modern, deep wells.

Though we learn much about life in Daggett, many features of Dix's life continue to intrigue. We wonder why in the following Dix makes no mention of his mother and why he never introduces his sister, Mary, who lived at the ranch. He also omits several unusual people, such as famed naturalist of the day John Burroughs, who passed through the ranch. As discussed in the Epilogue, perhaps manuscripts coming to light in the future will soothe our tantalized curiosity on such matters. Meanwhile, I cannot testify to the accuracy of many of Dix's stories. In a major way of looking at it, this is not local history with the *i*'s dotted and the *t*'s crossed but one man's view of an area's final transition from a frontier to civilization. It is a story through the colored glass of a resident's mind, and Dix's version comes freighted with all that implies. Yet for that, the accounts are all the more authentic, written, not by a historian, but by a man who was there, involved, sometimes hotly, with the people and events swirling about him.

READERS INTERESTED in further explorations of frontier Daggett, of the surrounding Mojave Desert, and of the characters striding through their dusty past will find abundant material in the bibliography below.

A good place to start would be W. Storrs Lee's lyrical *The Great California Deserts*. In pulling together the history of California's deserts, Lee shows how various forces shifted over the decades to create our positive view of America's arid lands. Giving Daggett's context the John McPhee treatment, David Darlington offers *The Mojave*. Clifford Walker's scholarly but eminently readable *Back Door to California* traces human activity in the Mojave from the Ice Age to the present. Edmund C. Jaeger ably surveys the natural history of the region with *The California Deserts*. From the other pole, Peter Reyner Banham's *Scenes in America Deserta* takes a rogue's view of the Mojave. Seeing it in terms of modern art, the English critic produces an unsettling aesthetic and a promising philosophy of landscape.

More specifically as to Daggett, Catherine Banker's thesis, "A Structural History," concentrates on the story of the town's Old Stone Hotel. However, in the process she gives a concise and informative overview of Daggett, together with maps of the town and the area. Valuable from a personal angle is Patricia Keeling's *Once upon a Desert*. Her collection of old-timers' remembrances about the Mojave includes many tales about Daggett's wily ways and the people mentioned below. However, no one is likely to match the intensity of Carita Selvas's "Life on the Desert," a brief but chromatic glimpse at Daggett's vice and fierce, tattooed Indians wandering the streets. Finally, readers will find that Dennis G. Casebier's well-documented *Goffs and Its Schoolhouse*, an excellent history of a little Mojave town one hundred miles east of Daggett, plays an intriguing counterpoint to Dix's reminiscences.

As to the Van Dykes themselves, John C. Van Dyke's *Autobiography* includes visits to the ranch and has much to say about the Van Dyke family and its proud background. My own *Theodore Strong Van Dyke* explores Theodore Strong Van Dyke in his dual role as writer and judge in a rambunctious boom town.

Concerning the text offered here, despite his sharp, native talent, Dix (1879-1952) was not a professional writer. His pages come studded with creative spellings and original grammar. He has a passion for the passive voice and a near addiction to the past perfect tense. Dix sometimes uses "he" with an abandon that leaves the referent far behind. In the editing of the following, I have not hesitated to smooth out many—but not all—such places. The foremost idea is to strike a balance between offering a readable text and retaining the witty, wayward, and down-home flavor of Dix's writing. I have followed Keeling in regularizing the spelling of names.

Judging from internal evidence, as well as from what we know about Dix, he probably wrote these reminiscences in his later years. The location of the original manuscript, if it still exists, is not known. Throughout 1953, most of what appears below ran in the *Barstow Printer Review*, the local newspaper, as a series of articles published on Thursdays and bearing such kindred titles as "The Pioneer Story" and "Pioneers." Dix's entry in the Select Bibliography under "The Pioneer Story" lists the dates of these pieces. However, the newspaper articles not only sometimes scramble some of Dix's passages, they rather rudely chop up Dix's prose into uniform chunks. Thus, in the newspaper version Dix's stories often end in midstream, to be continued in the next installment one or two Thursdays hence. I have changed some of these rigid divisions, but I've kept others to reflect the roughness of the original.

In light of such circumstances, we are fortunate to have what is believed to be a copy of Dix's original manuscript, a single-spaced, albeit incomplete, onionskin typescript in the holdings of the Mojave River Valley Museum at Barstow. Beginning on page 5 and ending on page 65, this manuscript is missing a title page, along with pages 1-4, 31, and 50. It is missing all or portions of the material found in the *Barstow Printer Review* pieces for April 16, April 23, August 20, August 27, October 15, and October 22.

The text below, then, is a blending of the onionskin manuscript with the newspaper articles. For example, the concluding story concerning the disastrous Harmony Club picnic appears as the last piece in the newspaper series, dated December 10. Though as printed in the newspaper this does not appear in the onionskin manuscript, material related to the story occurs both on page 55 of Dix's manuscript and in the newspaper articles for October 29 and November 5. To avoid confusion and to end Dix's story on a conclusive note, the final piece blends these versions into one whole. Dix's typescript is continuous. The divisions, headings, and notes are created by the editor for the convenience of the reader.

DAGGETT

1 THE ARRIVAL ✦ It was a shabby, dreary-appearing little village of three or four dozen houses, sprawled out on both sides of the railway tracks. Most of the houses were shacks built of rough, unpainted boards stood on end, with slats nailed over the cracks. The more pretentious ones were lined inside with cheesecloth, with wallpaper stuck on with flour paste. Beside the kitchen door stood a whiskey barrel with one end knocked out to serve as a reservoir. A pumping plant in the riverbottom piped water to the houses. However, it only flowed two hours each day, and during the remainder the house dwellers had to depend upon the barrel.

Three stores, three saloons, two Chinese restaurants, two dismal-appearing rooming houses with beds for four bits, two livery corrals with an assortment of old plugs and dilapidated rigs, a drugstore, a butcher shop, two or three gamblers, and three shop-worn prostitutes comprised the "commercial interests" of the incipient metropolis. An old horse, a pig, and some curs wandered hopefully about. Scattered over the village a few stunted, disconsolate-looking trees appeared to be abandoning the struggle for existence.

In front of Old Mike's saloon a carefully nurtured pepper tree flourished. Here each day, a gang of "old stiffs" hopefully lingered, waiting for a "live one" to come along and set up the drinks. "The Pepper Tree Club" they were derisively labeled by the other saloons and their habitués.

There was little profit in the members of the club, but Old Mike did not care. He liked to loaf and chat with them and never objected to unprofitable loafers, as long as they did not make a nuisance of themselves. A "live one" blowing a stake could begin at Mike's, but when he got drunk and noisy, he had to take his money elsewhere to blow in. Mike would not tolerate drunks.

All about lay a parched and arid desert. The gray, sterile-appearing soil was littered with stones and scantily clothed with a sparse growth of creosote and sage bushes. The nearby riverbed was a barren stretch of sand. Except in flood time, the water flowed far beneath the surface. To the eastward stretched a great level valley bounded on all sides by ranges of barren mountains. The farthest appeared gloomy and desolate, but the brilliant hues of the nearby Calico Mountains scintillated in the sunshine and formed a gorgeous border beneath the emerald sky.

Down the village street plodded a small team of mules drawing a light wagon in which rode an elderly man and a youth. It was the only traffic that day, and the strangers attracted attention.

"Who's those galoots?" queried a loafer.

"Why, ain't you heard?" replied Old Mike. "They're going to start a farm and irrigate it with the Wind and Water Ditch."

"Haw, haw, haw," guffawed the bunch.

"Where'd those durn fools come from?"

"Los Angeles," rejoined Mike.

"Jack Duane knows the old man. Says he's a smart feller. He is a lawyer and writes books."

"He won't be so damned smart after he's tried farming awhile," ventured another listener.

"I heered," piped up an old miner, "that the young feller said he was going to stay here until he had to walk out."

"He'll do it all right, if he farms long enough," observed another.

It was an odd pair. A cultured, intellectual scholar, who had never labored for a livelihood. He had been a lawyer in Minnesota until failing health caused him to abandon his profession at the age of thirty-three. After coming to Southern California for his health, he partially supported his family by his skill in hunting deer and other game, with which the land then teemed.

Now for diversion, he read the works of ancient writers in the original Greek and Latin. Sixty years old and in frail health, he had come to the desert to make a farm.

The son was twenty-two years old, tall, active, and sound in wind and limb. During the preceding three years, he had spent much time roaming about, riding on the truss rods beneath freight trains, in the night sprawled upon the top of passenger coaches, and sometimes carrying his bedroll on dusty roads. He had camped in the hobo jungles and mingled with the jungle buzzards, bundle stiffs, professional wanderers, gay cats, and the flotsam and jetsam that drifts about America. He labored on ranches and in construction camps and worked at various lowly jobs. His father had not discouraged this mode of life, deeming it a better education than poring over books. But he was intensely disgusted when he learned that his son had imbibed a belief in Socialist doctrines and descanted on the wrongs of labor. Occasionally, the father and son would engage in acrid debate, when the elder in exasperation would declare:

"You just wait until you get some men working for you. Then you will get some different ideas."

Along with it all, however, the son acquired a fierce determination to be no man's slave, to in some way gain a living, meager though it might be, where he would not need to knuckle down to anyone, nor shape his beliefs and opinions to conform to those of others. Maybe he was just naturally an individualist. This trait helped much in keeping him contented during the many years of arduous toil and scant income that were to come. Now, in December 1901, he had come with his father to the desert to revive an abandoned irrigation project and farm lands upon which others had failed. He came to spend a few years and remained a long lifetime. But he did not then know that. To youthful minds, how bright the future seems:

> With what gay hopes
> life's flowery pathway is strewn,
> But callous truth dispels
> the dreams and fantasies of youth.

Long ago a great lake covered the site of the Calico Mountains, and rock hounds now garner fragments of petrified wood that once grew along its shores. Along came one of nature's stormy times. Volcanic fires rent and tore the land, burned it, churned it, and threw it about. When quiet returned to the earth, the lake was gone, and in its place stood a high range of volcanic mountains. Nature, by its mysterious alchemy, had stained and tinted them with a medley of brilliant colors and stored treasures of gold, silver, and borax in the deep fissures of the mountains.

For fifty years the great Spanish Trail from New Mexico to California formed a passageway along the foot of the mountains for a motley crowd of adventurers, immigrants, and gold seekers. None had been foolish enough to waste time seeking treasure in the lava. Did not everyone know that riches were not found in such formations?

Finally, a wandering prospector who knew no better discovered that rich veins of silver lay embedded in the sides of the deep canyons that cleaved the face of the range. For many years, a horde of men explored, dug, and mined the silver ores. On the side of the mountain they built a town, constructed mills, and pumped water from the valley below with steam boilers heated with creosote bush. Calico became a boom town, with plenty of easy money and optimism thicker than winter fog.*

Extending southward toward Daggett lies a fertile, level valley.† Some of Calico's optimistic souls conceived a magnificent project for diverting water from the underflow of the Mojave River and irrigating the land near Calico. This was when Calico was enjoying its greatest prosperity, and as in all boom mining camps, the inhabitants believed the treasure hoarded within the mountain was limitless. In line with this, every other prospect had rosy hues.

In 1885, the Silver Valley Land & Water Company was incorporated. Lowry Silver, one of the discoverers of Calico, was an incorporator, and the project was given his name.

Water problems always appear simple to the novice. If you desire water, you just go and get it. That's all there is to it. This is a fine

---

*Artfully restored and now a county park, this jumbled mountain town is well worth a visit.
†Daggett is named for early resident John Daggett, who laid out the town and later became California's lieutenant governor.

theory when the water is above ground, but when it lies beneath the surface, it becomes a sly, mysterious, elusive thing. There, it follows devious trails that at best can only be guessed. The would-be water developers understood mining, but few of them knew ought of underground streams. Besides, back then hydraulic engineering was a rather crude science learned largely by experience instead of from poring over books and learning from the experience of others.

2 SCAMS, AND MORE SCAMS ✦ A FOOL'S DREAM: "THE WIND AND WATER DITCH" ✦ COMFORT IN THE FLOWING BOWL ✦ After several years of desultory efforts and the spending of much money, the Company had conducted some surveys, drilled a few test holes, and excavated a canal half a mile long on the north side of the river. None of the developers knew what to do or how to raise more money to complete the project. Before this time, T. S. Van Dyke had regained his health and become renowned as a versatile writer, well-informed on various subjects. Instead of hunting, he now bought his meat in the butcher shop and only pursued wild game for recreation. He was reputed to be a competent hydraulic engineer who had been successful in launching and constructing one large irrigation project. He was an authority on all subjects pertaining to irrigation. The developers sought his aid. After an investigation, he induced them to sell their holdings to a new company and to accept irrigation water for compensation. Mr. Van Dyke was given stock in the old company, for which the new company was to give water rights.

He had always desired a farm, and now he believed his hopes would be realized. Professional men are prone to believe that they are gifted with a special ability denied most farmers and that with a piece of land they can just achieve wonders. Maybe it was because his ancestors had been dwellers of the open places, and the ancestral urge to abandon the city and return was surging within him.

In 1893, the Southern California Development Company was organized. Those were the good old days when promoters could nail the Jolly Roger to the masthead and go cruising for victims undeterred by harassing laws designed to save the trusting ones from being swindled of their money. Promoters could use almost any deceit to obtain funds from deluded investors and could do almost as they pleased with the money.

The Mojave is a strange stream, unlike any other. In past ages, when the land had a wet climate, the river gouged a deep trench across the desert. As rainfall diminished and the stream flow lessened, stones and gravel gradually filled the trench over which the flood waters flowed. The gravel beds absorb much of the river's water, and during dry periods the water slowly flows beneath the surface. During dry periods, at Daggett the water flowed sixty feet below the surface of the river channel, but several miles upstream a granite reef extended across the river course and formed a submerged dam that backed up the underflow and caused a portion of it to run on the surface at all times.

The new company began operations during an acute financial depression, but the law then laid no restraints on their methods. They proceeded to issue grandiloquent and flamboyant advertising as the construction work began. A steam dredger scooped a great canal a mile long below the reef. Above a great wooden flume 2,100 feet long was laid fifteen feet below the river's surface. With mule teams the great canal was extended to Daggett, and from there a smaller one extended six miles farther. When completed, there were ten miles of canal constructed along the gravelly slope of the mountains, and the flume delivered into it only a very small fraction of the water needed to fill it.

Before the canal's completion, they affixed a water gate to the outlet of the underground flume, the lower half of which was a tight aqueduct. When the gate was closed, the water backed up until it flowed upon the surface of the river. Prospective investors were always brought from Los Angeles by train. Before their arrival the water gate was raised, and they beheld a large stream of water flowing in the great canal. After that, it was easy to persuade them to buy shares of stock and irrigation water.

East of Daggett lay a great valley of fertile land, and the ridiculous claims of the promoters that the canal was destined to irrigate most of it seemed quite reasonable. Why not? Those being duped could

see the water flowing. Why concern oneself about watersheds, rainfall, and stream flow? At any rate, at that time there were no statistics
concerning such subjects, and few people ever heard of such things.

Thirty years before, a youth had been a cowboy along the Mojave
River. In 1924, when a very old man, he wrote a long legal brief in
which he said:

> Many men in different times have conceived grand schemes and had
> wonderful visions of the possibilities of the Mojave River. Whether it is
> the majestic sweep of the wonderful panorama of the plains and moun-
> tains under a blue and cloudless sky, or whether it is the experience of
> seeing some water where none had been seen for hundreds of miles, or
> whether it is the climate that fires the imagination, or whether it be the
> indomitable spirit of man attempting the impossible, suffice it to say
> that both man and Creator have attempted to spread the water of this
> river over a greater stretch of territory than the initial supply produced
> in the mountain watershed will warrant.

The deceptive operations of the new company filled Mr. Van Dyke
with wrath and dismay, but there was nothing he could do about it.
He had thrown in his lot with the old company, and with them he
hoped to get water from the new canal. This was in compensation for
the water rights they had surrendered.

Flung over the desert for one hundred miles, a great range of
mountains lies sprawled. The Newberry Mountains east of Daggett
form a huge spur jutting out from the main range into the great valley.
Its sharp, serrated peaks are a ragged border along the skyline. Deep,
precipitous niches cleave its steep slopes of red lava down which the
storm waters course. When the sun is setting, shadows fill them with
deep-blue hues that form a somber background for the rosy colors of
the ridges illuminated by the sun's rays. Low down on the flanks and
sixty feet above the valley's floor, the canal ended, and here some more
fine promotion work was done.

The promoters laid out a townsite and garlanded it with white
stakes. They erected several houses, a small hotel, a schoolhouse, a
post office, and a real estate office. The wife of a company official was

named Minnie. She was honored by having the town and adjacent railway station named Minneola. The Minneola Town Company was incorporated and shares of stock issued.

The promoters circulated more flamboyant advertising. A well-written prospectus depicted a glorious future for the newborn metropolis. Far back on the desert, beyond the Newberrys, lies a large deposit of iron ore. No use has ever been found for it, but now the confiding ones were told that a hydroelectric plant would be constructed at Minneola and the iron brought down and smelted with electricity. Minneola was destined to become "the Pittsburgh of the West."

In 1898, a river freshet coming a month ahead of time broke into the unprotected head of the canal and sent a muddy stream coursing through Minneola. This puddled the gravelly ditch with mud so that the bottom did not leak so much, and it became possible to coax a small stream through after the flood subsided. It also gave the canal company an opportunity to collect payment from purchasers of water rights who had contracted to pay when water was delivered to them. They resisted, but the company sued them, produced witnesses who swore that they had hunted ducks upon the defendant's lands, and judgment was given to the Company.

A few hopeful souls tried to raise crops. The hardy ones lingered through the spring windstorms, but the coming of summer finished them. The natural condition of the soil and climate were so different from anything they had ever experienced that they could not understand them. The Salvation Army was contemplating the establishment of farm colonies for the regeneration of city paupers. They sent an officer who had long lived in India and was supposed to have knowledge of irrigation farming under similar climatic conditions. He planted some experimental crops and lingered for a while. It was too much for him. He fell from grace, sought comfort in the flowing bowl, and disappeared.

In five years' time the project lay abandoned and plastered with the liens of creditors. The Company was bankrupt and in such bad odor that no more money could be raised. Water still flowed in the canal, and trees lined the water's edge. Moss grew in the water, and retarding the flow, formed ponds that afforded grand duck hunting.

The locals derisively dubbed the enterprise "the Wind and Water Ditch." They jeered at anyone who even suggested that the land could produce a crop of any kind. For years it was regarded as a fool's dream, and even the creditors did not deem their claims worth sustaining and allowed them to lapse.

3 DREAMS AND WOES ♦ A NOSE IN THE MUCK ♦ A HARASSING FATHER ♦ The old Silver Valley Land & Water Company still owned the water rights and the water-bearing lands where the canal had its beginning. The investors had never been paid. The few who had valid claims against the canal gladly accepted trivial sums for them.

Mr. Van Dyke now came forth with a new plan for irrigation. Said he:

> There is plenty of water still flowing in the canal to irrigate a large acreage adjacent to Daggett. I know how to farm that land. I can raise crops on it. Everything consumed in that locality is shipped from the Coast by rail. The freight rate on hay is $4 a ton. What better protective tariff could anyone want? I can make enough money raising alfalfa to revive the project and demonstrate that farming can be profitable.
>
> There is nothing the matter except that a lot of fools have hoodooed the whole thing, and no one has faith in it. As soon as I demonstrate that the land is all right, we can raise all the money we need.

He had never done any real farming but during a long period had roamed about and had closely observed the efforts of others. Anyone who does this long enough will delude himself with the belief that he is a master of the art. He had written a book telling how to irrigate farmlands and for many years had contributed to various magazines telling others how to farm and irrigate. He had acquired a wide reputation as an authority upon agriculture and irrigation. Experts were scarce in those days, and he was as competent as any. He was so cocksure, so sanguine, that he convinced three of the original investors and persuaded them to join him in the effort. They were to furnish funds to maintain him until the anticipated profits rolled in. And now the little mules were conveying him and his son for their first inspection of the proposed farm.

While the great canal was building, some optimistic beings had incorporated the Daggett Land Company and under the Desert Land Act had filed a claim on 320 acres of land adjoining the town. They attempted to farm a portion of it. They cleared brush, made ditches, and smoothed a lot of land. One mesquite tree, three cottonwoods, and a few scattered alfalfa plants survived. The company owed $500 to a bank and gladly offered to surrender the land if the note was not paid.

The land lay along the lower edge of a great detrital slope that extended upward for miles and ended on the flanks of a granite mountain. On its side two knobs of red lava and the remains of an ancient borax lake bed showed that, like the rest of the land, it had long ago been churned up. The soil was largely a mixture of sand, gravel, and small stones. The same material was later hauled long distances to ballast railway tracks.

It was a warm, still day. Wintry weather had not arrived. The warm sunshine coming through a cloudless sky was cheering and inspiring. What finer climate could one desire? All about in every direction the endless array of mountains extended to the far, distant horizon. How clear the air was and how invigorating! The land appeared fertile. Did they not know that the finest of citrus fruits were grown upon the gravel slopes on the other side of the great mountains that enclosed the desert? The two newcomers were destined to learn the difference, but they did not know it now.

The first problem was cleaning the canal so that water would flow through it in the summer. It had a grade of 8/2 inch a hundred feet.* Just right if the canal was full of water. Toiling in rubber boots, Dix and his father drove a plow through the tule beds, tearing loose the roots and yanking them out by hand. There was a foot of mud in the canal. By dragging a V-shaped scraper through it, the mud

*Although Dix's exact meaning is unclear here, he is referring to the slope of the canal, which carried water by gravity to the ranch.

was pushed sideways and a small sub ditch four feet wide and a foot deep was made. Thereafter, occasional dragging of the scraper with a team threw aside the mud until grass growing on the banks firmly held them.

The flume beneath the river had been wrongly constructed, and the roof of the lower half depended upon spikes to sustain it. These had rusted, and in one place the flume had caved in. But not enough dirt had fallen to stop the flow of water. Before the ditch cleaning was finished, enough more caved in to stop the flow of water. Here was an appalling situation, and one that two months before would have prevented their coming, but nothing could daunt them now. They had become enthralled by the illusive mystic charm of the desert. A thing that fills one with a spirit of exaltation and imbues many with the belief that they are destined to perform great achievements.

Who can define the lure and enchantment of the desert? Many have felt it, but none have ever been able to explain it or the reason for it. The overwhelming appeal may be the brilliant, tinted skies and the eternal sunshine or the marvelous colors of the desert landscape with its constantly varying shades and shadows scintillating in the sun. Maybe it is the boundless, vast panorama of hills and mountains that constantly unfurls before the traveler that fires the imagination and induces mankind to attempt to perform impossible feats. Yet all over the great desert one finds evidence of futile hopes: abandoned mines, mill sites, land clearings, orchards, deserted homesteads, and the ruins of farms and other enterprises that were started and abandoned.

In March the father wrote to Mr. Dieterle, one of his supporters in Los Angeles:

> For three weeks I have had no water. For the past two weeks I have had my nose in the muck of the canal and have cut out a sub ditch through three miles of it. It needs a vast amount of constant care to keep it free of moss and the encroachment of vegetation. The sides are lined with willows and cottonwoods so large that we get all of our fenceposts while Quatomotes (a large evergreen bush) and other water growths are thick as hair on a dog.
>
> The main thing now is to demonstrate, not that the land is good, but

that a stream big enough to irrigate anything can be got through and maintained in hot weather. I am not a bit discouraged or I would not stay here. I made an ass of myself bragging to Dr. Jarvis. In the future I will keep still until I do something.

Long before the Van Dykes came, a hardy pioneer had established a small ranch in the riverbottom at the canal heading and had irrigated it from perennial streams then flowing in the river. His notices appropriating water from "the South and North branches of the Mojave River" are in the County archives. Long ago, a flood swept away his farm, and later the underground flume drained down the water. Now the underground reef athwart the river channel backed up the water until it again flowed on the surface. The upper end of the canal was fifteen feet deeper than the surface of the dry river channel, and as the water level rose, it began percolating through the sides of the canal. A shallow ditch was scooped in the river channel, and the small stream now flowing in it was conducted into the canal. By constant effort, a small stream was coaxed through the canal to the new farm beyond Daggett.

In March the strangers were busy preparing land for the irrigation of anticipated crops. The weather was still fine, and they were undaunted by the doleful prophecies of the natives that they would have no water when hot weather came. Along came Mr. Frank Parish, homeward bound for his mesquite and salt grass ranch in the riverbottom at Camp Cady, twenty miles downstream.* He tarried long enough to bestow advice.

"You fellers might just as well quit. This land ain't no count for nothing. There is a borax mine up at the foot of that mountain yonder. That stuff has been washed down here and has pizened this land.

---

*Major James H. Carleton of the First Dragoons established Camp Cady in 1860 to protect travelers from the many Indian attacks plaguing the Mojave desert. Intermittently garrisoned, the camp was moved a half mile west in 1868, then abandoned in 1871. For further details, see Waitman's history of the camp and Keeling (60–63, map 58). In *The Battle at Camp Cady* and *Carleton's Pah-Ute Campaign*, two brief but admirable works of scholarship, Casebier offers intimate views of military life at Cady and the surrounding area.

Other people have tried to raise stuff here, and they had to quit, and you will, too."

His remarks were somewhat blighting, but the unbelievers were later cheered when they learned that he was an old soak who ten years before, to get away from booze, had begun a solitary life. And that now he drank only alkali water with daily doses of patent medicine to counteract the alkali's evil effects. He was the possessor of a bilious, irascible, and pessimistic nature. His brother was reputed to be the only man who had ever been legally hanged in Lincoln County, Nevada, and many felt that the law had not done its full duty.

Five acres were deeply plowed, alfalfa seed scattered over it by hand broadcasting and harrowed in. This method was all right on the Coast, where each night the fog rolled in and dew moistened the land. Here, it just made a porous bed of loose earth the winds dried out. A few scattered plants sprouted, but they soon gave up struggling for life.

The ranchers laid out a small garden with meticulous care. The furrows were marked with a string stretched taut between two stakes and gouged out with a hoe. They ran water into the furrows, dropped in seed, and raked in loose soil to cover the seed. The soil should have been firmly packed over the seed, but the Van Dykes did not know that then, and the garden shared the fate of the alfalfa seed.

The son did most of the work, while the father harassed him with instructions.

"I want this done right." He complained, "I don't want to show anything that I have to make apologies for."

He never had to. No one ever suspected that it was a vegetable garden, though two years later some of the seed grew.

4 JEERS AND SPREES ♦ THE JUDGE GOES TO LOS ANGELES ♦ "A GREAT SAND BLAST" ♦ HOLIDAYS ♦ Old Mike owned a fine driving mare and a good buggy in which he occasionally drove about. It was his only extravagance. Mike was very proud of his mare. She had a colt sired by a fine stallion. An astute whiskey drummer, after spending part of a day admiring the colt and praising its fine qualities, offered $500 for it. He did not get the colt but easily sold Mike a six months' supply of whiskey. Both parties parted in good cheer.

Mike occasionally drove to the ranch and offered advice, the rejection of which caused him much disgust. He was really anxious to see the strangers succeed, and being long a resident of the desert, he deemed his advice of value. With the passing of spring, he dolefully predicted that no water would flow through the canal in July. It had not done so before the flume caved in, and it did not seem possible that puny efforts could work a miracle with the diminished stream. It did, though.

One day in disgust the son ejaculated, "That damned ditch makes me sick."

"It will make you a lot sicker before summer is over," replied the village butcher.

Long afterwards, the butcher started a ranch nearby that gave him plenty of sick spells and depleted his bank account.

Among themselves the natives jeered and ridiculed the belief that crops could be raised upon the sterile soil and prophesied a dismal failure, but they kept their opinions to themselves. They were a kindly, generous, and friendly people. They were courteous to the strangers and veiled their skepticism with expressions of good wishes and gladly rendered any favors that could help the Van Dykes. Many of them had long lived on the frontier and had come from older mining camps in California and Nevada. They were not a pious people. A preacher had once climaxed a week of revival services in the schoolhouse by asking all who were saved to stand up. None stood.

Then after a fervid exhortation, he appealed to all those who desired to be saved to stand. None stood.

This broke the poor preacher. He left town the next day after gloomily remarking that Daggett was the worst town he had ever been in. This was libel. Most of the inhabitants were industrious, honorable men who paid their debts, kept their word, and were willing to help their fellows. Most of them were poor and toiled for meager wages, but it was always easy to collect money for anyone who was in need.

It was a man's town, a rendezvous for miners, and an outfitting point for roamers of the desert who came from many distant places to get supplies and perhaps have a spree. Most of those who sinned did so openly, and their frailty was regarded with charity. This, however, was not so if one became intoxicated and went looking for trouble. Then it was open season on him, and blame was seldom laid on the one who gave him what he was looking for.

"Walk away from trouble if you can. If the other fellow has to have it, give it to him with anything you can get your hands on."

This was the good, old pioneer rule, and in frontier courts it had more effect than written laws. In such cases, witnesses were often difficult to locate and usually testified that they had fled without looking backward to see what happened. The minority of women in the town exercised little influence, but they were expected to deport themselves decorously, and they did so.

In April the father journeyed to Los Angeles after giving minute instructions for the planting of corn and beans.

"And don't you plant all of the seed. I want to plant some every two weeks so we will always have some ripening and ready to eat," he enjoined.

In a week he returned, expressing intense disgust for city life and vowing that never again would he wear a biled shirt and a stiff collar. He never did again. On learning that all of the corn and beans had been planted, he scowled at his son and wrathfully exclaimed,

"Confound you. Why could you not do what you were told? That stuff will all ripen in a heap, and we will not be able to use it. A lot of it will just go to waste."

Only one acre had been planted, but like those who sit by the fireside on winter nights and gloat over a seed catalog, the father had visions.

In this locality from June to March there is very little wind, but in springtime it is often a nuisance, though very strong winds are rare. This year there was an overdose of what Californians call "unusual weather." On many days it was necessary to wear goggles, and the winds did not cease with the advent of summer. It was the windiest year the strangers were to know and one long remembered. There were two or three times the normal amount of wind. The beans and corn grew, and on the eighteenth of May the corn was a foot high. Then a terrific gale struck Southern California and wrought great damage on the sea coast. On the desert, which was dry, it had all the fury of a great sand blast. Hills a mile distant were hidden from view. On the ranch everything planted was shaved off at the roots and killed. The wind even whipped the desert bushes about and stripped off most of their leaves.

The day after the wind, the ranch was a forlorn and dismal prospect. But the strangers gritted their teeth and prepared to replant. When some of the townsmen expressed sympathy and solicitously inquired what they intended to do now, they were rudely informed that "we ain't licked yet. We're going to stay right here until we learn whether this land is any good."

Again the fields were planted. This time several acres were put in. A dispute arose over the proper spacing of the melons.

"The vines must not be planted too close together," authoritatively declaimed the father. "In Minnesota I planted a field five feet apart and all I grew was vines. They covered the ground so thick that no melons grew. We have plenty of land. There is no use taking chances. I want to play safe."

He sure did. The scrawny, stunted little vines did not grow large enough to tangle with their fellows. Each one had to battle for life without fraternal help. Each was whipped about by the westerly winds and tangled into a long hank strung out easterly. However, they blossomed, and tiny melons formed and cheered the planters.

Again the winds came. On the desert there was then no Sunday observance except an occasional Sunday school meeting in the schoolhouse. The toilers worked ten or more hours every day in the week. It was just the old frontier mining camp custom that still prevailed. There was nothing else to do. Why loaf? There were, however, four holidays that were usually observed: St. Patrick's Day, the Fourth of July, Thanksgiving, and Xmas. People usually celebrated these with a baseball game during the day and a dance at night. On the Fourth, the day began auspiciously. The ballplayers and spectators gathered. It was customary to cheer the players with a bucket of water well diluted with whiskey donated by the saloons, but before they had time to develop a thirst, the wind came hurling clouds of dust and deposited dirt and sand in the bucket. The spectators fled, and the discomfited ballplayers sought refuge and solace in the saloons.

For three days and nights a dry, desiccating wind blew. On the second day, the leaves on the melon vines began turning black around the edges, and on the third day they looked as though scorched by a hot fire.

The father wrote to an associate in Pasadena:

My dear Mills,

I suppose you are wondering where I am at, but you are not wondering any more than I am. The severest windstorm of the season but one has just closed after lasting five days and nights at forty miles an hour. It has cleaned out most of the stuff at the ranch. Much has been done up before, three different plantings. But I had five acres of melons looking fine that grew three inches a day all last week and did the best with the mercury at 114°, when everyone told me they would burn up. Today they look so bad that I am going to replant the whole patch.

Muskmelons fared worst, cucumbers and all else the same. Alfalfa and sorghum were merely stopped and will go ahead, I think. But corn, melons, and such things got stunted so badly that they will amount to little. The wind blights because the air is so dry.

On the eighteenth of May the wind killed all young stuff above ground. I had muskmelons completely protected with mosquito netting, but they were all killed, desiccated standing up straight. There was no wilting or dying of the plant. It was simply dried out in position. Everyone says that the present season is the worst on record and that such a storm in July was never known before.

Nor in the next forty years was there another such season.

5 RUSTLING ◆ A MIRACLE ◆ A DELEGATION ◆ Despite all such tribulations, the two men kept a small stream of water flowing through the canal, and a small crop of melons ripened in September. They were very sweet and fine-flavored. The natives eagerly bought $75 worth. The borax mill on the canal paid $75 a month for using water from the canal. This was encouraging, and the planting of fall crops was begun with renewed faith.

On the Mojave Desert the finest weather of the year comes in October. The still, warm days and cool nights, together with the endless sunshine and brilliant skies, are cheering to the soul and imbue one with optimism and hope. A deep, underground reef of clay extends from the Calico Mountains, crosses the Silver Valley, and passes the Newberry Mountains. This forms a submerged dam that backs up the underflow of the Mojave River that here spreads under the valley floor. On the downriver side of the reef the water levels lie deep. On the upper the water is near enough to the surface to nourish a growth of brush and mesquite trees upon which the wind has heaped sand and formed many dunes, some quite high.

Near the Calicos the river has cut a wide trough down the valley. Here above the reef the water comes to the surface and flows in a perennial stream through a thousand acres robed in grass, brush, and trees. At long periods a destructive flood cuts a wide swath through them, but within a few years nature restores the jungle. This was an important stopping place on the Old Spanish Trail from New Mexico. Here all travelers lingered to rest before starting or arriving on the long trek over the desert to Las Vegas de Quintana (now the site of Las Vegas, Nevada). Later, when a military road to Arizona was established, it diverged from this point and continued on down the river. This point was known as the Forks of the Road. Until the building of railways, it was an important place.

On the north side of the river, some small fields of alluvial silt, laid down long ago by river floods, comprised the ranch of Jack Le Furgey. On the upper end a slough usually furnished water in springtime, but in summer and dry seasons water was pumped with a crude contraption modeled after those used in ancient Egypt. A great wheel lay on the ground with its vertical axle fixed rigidly in place. There were a dozen long spokes forked on the end around which ran a rope that turned a wooden roller. This turned a long canvas belt with wooden cleats nailed to it which pushed the water up a wooden trough. A horse was hitched to one spoke, the next went under his belly, and he was tied to the one in front. This was a very efficient machine for raising water a few feet. Most of the old Chinese vegetable gardens in California were located where they could be irrigated with similar pumps.

Jack had a small herd of cattle and some mustangs that rustled a living for themselves in the riverbottom and on the adjacent desert lands. In winter he gained an unsavory reputation by butchering cattle and peddling the meat. Cattle owners are suspicious creatures, and disparaging remarks were made regarding Jack's ability to distinguish cattle brands. He always scoffed at the aspersions and blithely went his way. In summer he cultivated a field of corn and melons. He had an industrious wife and two girls who were good riders and willing workers.

This windy year finished them. Jack ceased farming and gathered his horses and moved to Daggett and engaged in the livery business. Old Pap Medlam had long maintained a livery stable with a few decrepit horses and rigs. Old Mike bought this and rented it to Jack. They had long been close friends, but they finally disagreed on the question of rent, and Jack removed to the abandoned borax corral that had once sheltered the twenty-mule teams. This so soured Mike, who was stubborn-natured, he hired a manager and continued the livery, and now the town had three. From some place Mike secured an odoriferous old billy goat and added him to the stable.

"Mike, what have you got that goat for?" enquired Dix.

"Why, to keep sickness and disease away from the horses," replied Mike.

The son had never before heard of this ancient superstition, and the incredulity he manifested angered Mike.

"You domned fool you," he roared, "don't yez know anything at all? Anny wan ought to know that much."

The strangers planted twenty acres to grain and alfalfa. The fields were carefully furrowed and well irrigated. No seed grew between the furrows, but in them where the water flooded the seed grew thick.

In October the father again wrote to Mills:

> The new alfalfa is coming up, and so is the grain with it. The only trouble is an army of birds that will not bunch up so that I can rake them with a shotgun, and they are too wild for sure single shots with a .22 rifle.
>
> They eat an immense quantity as soon as it gets green. They can't be poisoned because they will not touch dry seed or grain. I have in five acres of the new stuff, and there will soon be too much for them. They have with the rabbits kept three acres down all summer.
>
> It has been a dry year here—such as never before known. Only one inch of rain in over a year and everything just starved out and crazy for green stuff.

The strangers had found much to comfort them in their new way of life. The son was the sole survivor of three, the others having died when he was a small child. While the father was naturally a kind and affectionate parent, this bereavement made him more indulgent. He had always been solicitous of the son's health, which was why he had not attended school in his childhood. By the age of nine, in some mysterious way he picked up the art of reading, and ever after he was a constant reader of various subjects. He now found much pleasure and joy in close association with his scholarly father, and it was consoling for him to learn that his son was contented with a frugal, toiling life and cared little for ease or spending money. And there had come a marvelous improvement in the father's health. For the last half of his life he had been burdened with sick headaches and insomnia. One summer on the desert ended this. Something about the dry, hot sunshine lasting months on end wrought a miracle. Now he slept soundly all night and awakened each morning refreshed and fit for another day of labor.

Mr. Le Furgey returned from a trip to San Bernardino, where he had made a futile effort to rent his ranch to a Chinese vegetable grower. Because of his verbosity, he bore the name of Windy Jack. The Chino patiently listened to a glowing description of the ranch and all the dollars a thrifty Chink could garner. Before Jack's time, when Calico was booming, some Chinese tried to raise garden truck there. The Chino was wise. He ended the interview by tersely saying,

"Too muchee hot, too muchee cold, too muchee wind, no grow."

"And," gloomily related Jack, "that damned Chink tole the whole story."

A delegation prevailed upon the father to become a candidate for the office of Justice of the Peace and departed, leaving him in a daze that lasted throughout the day. His own father had been a prominent man in the state of New Jersey, where his ancestors had dwelt for 200 years. Another son long after his death wrote of him:

> He sat in the trial of cases with his colleagues, heard quarrels and fought outside battles as before. (He was then a Justice of the Supreme Court of the state.) But law and lawyers, politics and politicians, with public and social life, were growing a little irksome for him. He was wearing on toward sixty. His dark hair and beard, that had earned him in early political days the sobriquet of "Black Hawk," had become thickly sprinkled with grey.[*]

Soon after, in 1868, he yanked up stakes, sundered all home ties, and with his wife and five sons moved to the frontier state of Minnesota. He tried to make farmers of his sons. They would have none of it. They all took kindly to books and qualified themselves for professions. Four of the sons became lawyers, one a medical doctor.

No doubt his son Theodore, while studying law and later pleading causes in court, dreamed of someday enjoying the prestige and honors of judicial office, of perhaps emulating his famous forebear, and now he gave his promise to become the Justice of the Peace in a squalid little village in the midst of the desert for the meager salary of $20 a month. During the remainder of his life, this petty office was to bring him much renown. Upon his death in 1923, his son succeeded him and the office remained in the family for forty years. But now he felt

---

[*]Here, Dix is quoting from *The Raritan,* the family history by his uncle John C. Van Dyke (78).

sheepish about it, and when his associate Dieterle visited the ranch, he enjoined him not to tell anyone in Los Angeles.

Later, a brother living in another state, upon hearing of it exclaimed, "My God, has he fallen that low?"

They had been living in a rented house in the village. Now they built a crude, three-room shack of rough boards. It was full of cracks that let in the wind and flies, but it was their home for the next five years. A hole scooped in the ground and filled with ditch water served for everything but drinking water. This was hauled from town.

6 OF RABBITS AND OLD SALLY AND CHRISTMAS IN THE DAGGETT DANCEHALL ♦ A MANIKIN MAKES A FACE ♦ A visitor took a photograph of the house. His daughter used it with a varied assortment of other shacks to illustrate a magazine article. She was considerate enough to omit the owner's name. It was merely labeled "The Desert Home of a Literary Recluse."

In November the father wrote Mills,

I have been expecting to send you a more cheerful report. Maybe the Thanksgiving dinner of beans from which I have just risen makes me a little blue. But as I look out the window and see the ranch daily getting more gray as of old, I feel depressed, although there is nothing really alarming about it.

The green of a month ago is all vanished before the birds and rabbits, and two patches of peas and three of radishes, once doing fine, are completely wiped out. From three acres of turnips I do not expect to get a mess for the table. In a few places where a tumbleweed has stuck fast and protected them, grain is six inches high and as nice as you would want to see. Everywhere else it is shaved off as with a pair of scissors.

The rabbits are the worst by far and will knock me out of a whole winter's pasture. The more stuff comes up, the more rabbits there are ready for it. I have caught a number in steel traps, but there are still too many. They come from miles away—jacks—and can't be found by day. I have followed their trail out two miles without finding any sign of their stopping.

The two-foot fence I put around the melon patch and which is sufficient all over California they soon learned to jump. It is probably because there is no feed. The total rainfall for the past year was one inch.

Everything has grown well since the wind stopped in September, and I would have had lots of peas and radishes if the rabbits had left them alone. One rabbit jumped the fence back out again with a steel trap on his leg. Some surveyors saw him several miles from here, still dragging the trap.

That is a tough story, but it is a fair sample of conditions here.

He failed to mention that a few days before he had been elected Justice of the Peace, nor does his letter indicate that it had a cheering effect.

Robert Findley Wilson was elected Constable. He was a Civil War veteran and the possessor of a gloomy, saturnine nature. He was reputed to be a bad man to start hostilities with and prone to belligerency. He demonstrated this one day. Armed with a club, he ordered a drunken, noisy rowdy to shut up and refrain from making more noise. The drunk poked a fist at Old Bob and was knocked down with the club and well beaten with it. After which Bob stalked off, not deigning to arrest him.

Dix left for a month's visit to the Coast. There, the whole land was robed in green. It seemed beautiful to him to see green grass everywhere. He had never before appreciated that, but now after a year in the desert he did. "Going inside" was the term by which the desert dwellers denote such a journey to the Coast.* Each letter from home told of devastation by the rabbits, and Dix returned and built a three-foot fence around the ranch. A few rabbits went under and over but not enough to cause much damage. The alfalfa and grain now thrived.

"What's happened while I was away?" Dix queried of the village butcher. "Anything?"

"Yes, Old Sally died."

"What ailed her?"

"Wore out, I guess."

Sally was a sorry-looking, bedraggled old hag who dwelt in a dilapidated, one-room shack on the edge of town. For eight years t'was

---

*The term continues to be used by residents of the Mojave Desert. They apply the opposite, "going outside," to leaving city areas and returning to the desert.

said she had not drawn a sober breath. The old-timers testified that she was the handsomest woman that ever came to Calico. Sin and dissipation had brought her to this dismal end.

Of all her admirers when she was in her prime, only one remained. Ol' Smitty was a competent horseshoer who occasionally came and shod the village horses. Then he dwelt with Sally, and when the horses were all shod, a drunken debauch ensued. After Sally's death, he disappeared and never returned.

Sally's demise left China Mary and Midget the only fillet de joys, except occasionally when one or two would come around payday at the borax mines and linger until the miners had spent their money. Mary was an old hag and Midget well on the way. Two years later in another town, she stirred a man to jealous frenzy, and he shot and killed her.

Another old man named Wilson gained a meager living by milking a few cows and peddling the milk in the village. With his old wife he lived beside his cow corral. A local gambler who owned a fancy house on the other end of town began the erection of a dwelling next to Mr. Wilson's domicile. The village wags told the old gentleman that this was going to be another fancy house.* The frantic old man raced about the town protesting to those he deemed influential citizens. They all solemnly assured him that nothing could be done. The poor old man was in a turmoil for over a month.

"I believe," said Old Bob, "that the Judge is a pretty durn smart man. I took a hobo down there who said he was a Greek section hand. I told the Judge the feller was lying. The Judge said he'd quick find out. He give the bo a Greek book and told him to read it. The bo did, and the Judge could understand him. It all sounded like Chinee to me."

A grunt came from Old Wooley, who arose and went into Alex's saloon. He had been the defeated incumbent. For fifteen years Judge Owens had presided over the court. On his death, Wooley was appointed to fill the remainder of the term. The disgruntled ones asserted that for years he had been the town bum and that he had been appointed only to furnish him with means of support. And that he

---

*That is, a brothel.

possessed only one virtue, and that was he could always be found either in Alex's saloon or in Midget's brothel. Also, he had irritated his detractors by dropping his former sycophancy and adopting a magisterial dignity coupled with an authoritative manner of dispensing wisdom.

From somewhere he enticed a rather young woman with a young son. He introduced her as his wife from whom he had separated before coming to Daggett. The unbelievers sniffed and opined that he had secured her through a matrimonial agency. The romance ended within one month, blighted by unfeeling merchants who declined to grant credit. One day Judge Wooley appeared with a badly scratched face seeking a loan to pay the lady's fare on the railway.

He got it, and she went.

Christmas was always celebrated in Alex's dancehall, a dilapidated old building across the street from his saloon. A community tree was bought and decorated by public subscription. People gathered mistletoe from the cottonwood trees growing in the riverbottom.

In the surrounding hills grew a small sage bush. The desert dwellers never knew it was a thing of beauty until long after when city slickers peddled it on the streets of Los Angeles, calling it Desert Holly from Death Valley. In time, the demand for it became so great that in various places it was threatened with extinction and laws were enacted to forbid the gathering of it.

It was customary to dispense presents by writing the recipient's name on them and laying them at the foot of the tree. After a short musicale and some recitations, candy and goodies were presented to each child and the presents distributed by calling the names written on them. After the festivities were ended and the children went home, the floor was cleared for a dance that lasted until daylight. Walter Olivier played "In the Good Old Summertime" and other tunes upon his harmonica, and the railway agent's wife pounded the piano. Every gentleman contributed one dollar for the musicians.

Alex was content with the patronage his bar received. At intervals when the dancing ceased, part of the men would troop over to his saloon for stimulating drink. Not so the ladies. If any had, no man would have danced with her. Some of the men might become too inebriated to dance. Then, unless they voluntarily left, their friends would lead them away. There was never any trouble. Any man that started any would have incurred the anger of the others. The old desert dwellers were invariably courteous and deferential to women. They frowned on any rowdyism in their presence.

Alex was a canny old Scotchman who loved a joke. On the wall behind the bar, he installed a small, wooden manikin, so arranged that when one stepped on a pedal beneath the bar, the manikin would roll its eyes and wag its jaw. A bibulous stranger on the end of a week's drunk called for a drink of whiskey. His hand shook so much that it was with difficulty that he raised the glass. As he did so, he saw that manikin making faces at him. The drunk's eyes bulged with terror:

"My God," he groaned, "I am gettin' thim again." (Delirium tremens.) Without drinking, he set down the glass and disappeared into the night.

7 WINDY JACK ♦ MOTHER PRESTON, PUGILIST ♦ QUICKSAND ♦
On January 17, 1903, the father wrote to Dieterle,

> If I can work out the necessary problems with the ditch, it will relieve me from what I dread more than anything—responsibility for other people's money. I can cuss the ditch and go to sleep at sundown.
>
> Not so with debt and responsibility. I can live without them. If I can't work out certain things within the next two years, I shall throw in the sponge, and when it is announced that even Van Dyke gave it up, there will be nothing worth squabbling over.

He had not lost confidence in himself, but he was beginning to entertain doubts about the land and was harassed with the problem of coaxing sufficient water through the canal. The alfalfa had furrows only three feet apart, the water had failed to percolate sideways, and now the alfalfa grew only in the furrows. The field was streaked with alternating ribbons of brown and green.

However, the strangers began the new year undismayed by their past tribulations and still determined to demonstrate that the land would produce some kind of a profitable crop. Circumstances now favored them. A small flood came down the river and flowed a long time and raised the water level enough to ensure an ample flow of irrigation water. The alfalfa fields were flooded, and the seed on the brown ribbons sprouted and grew. There was not much wind and no destructive ones.

Again the Van Dykes planted, coddled, and cared for various kinds of vegetables. The plants came up all right, but they seemed appalled by their surroundings. For a while they made little growth but seemed to take courage with the coming of warm weather. In many places the Judge marked individual plants whose progress he carefully watched. Each day he inspected them and returned to the house, and sitting in the scanty shade he fluently cursed everything and everybody:

"Of all the ornery, cussed problems I ever tackled, this is the worst," he would squawl.

"If it were not for my reputation, I would quit. After writing for twenty years and telling others how to farm, I am ashamed to admit that I am a failure."

The grain made a scanty crop, and the alfalfa grew slowly. During the season they got enough to feed two small horses and a milk cow. Four acres of alfalfa consisted almost entirely of small, stunted, yellow plants that grew a few inches high and stood still, undecided what to do about it.

In various places where the Judge had lived, he had grown a few vegetables for home use. It had been a hobby from which he derived much pleasure, and he acquired much lore, but it was of little use here. He still cherished hopes of eating fresh vegetables, but they were mostly illusions. His favorite kind of sweet corn yielded only barren cobs. Tomatoes, beans, and cucumbers bore promising blossoms, but they matured, withered, and fell without producing fruit. Irish potatoes ceased growth with hot weather. Sweet potatoes thrived during the heat and gave encouragement, but the harvest yielded only a few stringy roots.

The Judge discoursed eloquently upon the advantages of raising a crop of Hubbard squash and storing away a winter's supply. Baked squash, he vowed, was a tasty and nutritious dish. Mysteriously, squash bugs appeared and attacked the vines. He slaughtered them with bug poisons, and the vines bore a few blossoms, but nary a squash developed. In time to come, he was to learn how to garden in harmony with the natural conditions of the desert and to grow only things that would thrive and yield in constant, hot sunshine and dry air. But now he fumed and fretted and cursed while he endeavored to make the soil and crops conform to his ideas of propriety.

A crop of small watermelons and cantaloupes was raised. They were sweet and delicious and easily sold. Even the Navajo Indians and Mexicans toiling on the railway for one dollar a day and living in hovels built of old railway ties with a dirt roof and floor came to the ranch and eagerly bought them without haggling over prices. Yet by fall the Van Dykes' efforts appeared so fruitless that now the natives regarded them with pity. Their sympathetic comments caused the two farmers intense irritation, much more so than any jeers could have done. Dix, the son, had often been admonished that only fools got mad, and clever people controlled their tempers. Now the father almost choked with suppressed emotion when Hank Goodrich kindly informed him that he "felt very sorry for anyone who tried to farm in the desert." Hank meant well. He was a sterling character who had served through the Civil War and disdained a pension, vowing that he could support himself. Shortly before his death when old and feeble, he retired to the veterans' home.

The Judge's health was steadily improving. "This is the finest climate in California," he declaimed. "I am never going to live in a city again. I am going to stay here."

"I will be damned if I will ever again work for wages," replied Dix.

These vows were kept.

Windy Jack was relaxing beneath the veranda in front of Mother Preston's saloon.

"My boy," he observed to Dix, "you will never make any money farming in this country."

"I would not have a farm in this country if you gave it to me," Mother Preston muttered.

The words fell on unbelieving ears. Who were they to dispense wisdom? Windy Jack had failed, and so had others, but that proved nothing.

Mother Preston bore evil repute. She had been a brothel keeper in Calico and was now said to rob drunken customers. She possessed a sour, morose nature, a fighting heart, and great physical strength. Short and chunky, with broad shoulders and powerful arms, she was a dangerous antagonist in a rough-and-tumble fight. No man in his senses desired a contest with her.

Mr. Jack Mahoney, while on one of his periodic sprees, paused in front of her saloon to make some scurrilous comments upon her shady past. She ignored his nasty aspersions, and Jack continued down the street to Alex's place. There was no diversion there. After imbibing another drink, he thought of some more information to bestow upon Mother. The old desert saloonkeepers were a hardy breed, inured to much verbal abuse from drunken customers. Jack presumed upon this.

If sober, he would not have dared to antagonize her. Now fortified with another drink and without any premonition of coming disaster, he returned and launched more insults. Like a spider after a fly, the tigress bounded from her lair. One smashing blow laid her traducer on his back. Then standing astraddle of him, she flailed her victim with both fists while he screamed with agony and kicked with both feet. The weather was warm. The pugilist wore only one garment. This, in his futile resistance, Jack kicked up about her waist while the spectators howled with glee. For a long time this episode was a standing joke.

When sixty years old, Mother gave a sober man an unmerciful beating. This by the simple expedient of wrapping one arm about his neck and clasping his head against her bosom while she punched his face. She finally met her first defeat in a contest with a business rival who belabored her with a piece of railway air hose with an iron coupling on the end. She sued for damages. She won a $1,500 judgment. Her lawyer kept all of it for his fee. She wrote him a vituperative letter and called him everything she could think of. The lawyer, Frank Daley, afterwards County Judge, was quite a wag and took great pleasure in exhibiting the letter.

She removed to the new town of Ludlow and acquired a saloon, store, lodging house, and restaurant. After eighteen years of gathering and hoarding wealth, she retired to her native France, where she soon died. Relatives inherited the results of her thrift. In the desert she became a tradition long remembered.

When the spring flood subsided, the son Dix did a fool thing. He endeavored to drive a horse with a cart across the river channel. He knew nothing of quicksand and selected a wide place above the canal heading where the water was shallow. He later learned to select narrow places where the water ran deep. He often had to strip off his clothes and first wade across and back before attempting to lead a saddlehorse over. But now in his ignorance he nonchalantly started across. Luck favored him, and he encountered no miry spots until close to the opposite bank. There the horse bogged and rolled on its side. The horse knew nothing of quicksand and, panic-stricken, gave up. Dix was badly frightened. Gruesome tales of human beings engulfed and sucked down in quicksands flashed through his mind as he hastily stumbled to the shore. He could not possibly have sunken more than knee deep, but he did not know that.

On the bank he found a pack outfit sufficient for several burros. The flood had undermined the bank and carried away some things. It looked like the unfortunate owner had been asleep, and the flood coming down in the night had overwhelmed and drowned him. Finding an axe, Dix chopped enough brush to build a causeway out to the horse and got it and the cart ashore. Gathering the pack outfit, he traversed the north bank to a ford opposite the town. Searching the pack, he found a letter to a Walter Scott written by his wife. After some fruitless inquiries, Old Mike informed Dix,

"That was the young fellow who came in here last fall and told me he had some rich gold ore in Death Valley and that he was going to send it in by the borax teams and ship it by express. Don't you remember? You heard him."

Dix remembered. Mysterious Scott, some had dubbed him. He had no cronies and traveled alone at unexpected times between Daggett and Death Valley, sometimes afoot and sometimes with burros.

John Sturnacle was an old-timer who lived in the riverbottom above the canal heading. A large tract enclosed with a fence made a pasture, and his small herd of cattle rustled for a living along the river. Selling firewood, pasturing stock, and selling a few cattle furnished a meager living for John, his wife, and three small kids. He was another Civil War veteran who disdained a pension until eighty years of age and feeble. Then he received $3,000 back pay. He solved the mystery of the packs:

"Scott," he said, "came in from Death Valley when the river was up. He yanked the packs off and turned the burros loose. They would not leave. They have been pastured at my place. Scott waded the river and came to my house and borrowed five dollars and went to Los Angeles."

8 MORE ABOUT "DEATH VALLEY SCOTTY" ♦ MURDER IN THE BUCKET OF BLOOD SALOON ♦ THE TOWN'S EVIL REPUTA-TION ♦ These were primitive times. Scott had little cause to worry about his packs. Someone would care for them. Dix did. That fall Scott returned with his attractive young wife, reclaimed his chattels, and for a time camped in the riverbottom. He was a stout, husky young fellow and thought nothing of walking alone over 160 miles of desert to Death Valley carrying scanty rations.

"I can walk forty miles a day for eight days and carry my grub," he boasted to Dix.

It sounded like bombast, but others confirmed his statement. In later years, he gained much renown and became famous under the pseudonym of "Death Valley Scotty."* In his old age he became fat

---

*Sobriquet of Walter Perry Scott (1872?-1953), a much celebrated desert character who kept secret the location of his fabulously rich gold mine. Among other showy acts, he built a castle in Death Valley. His money actually came from a Chicago millionaire who found Scott's antics amusing.

The *Los Angeles Times* demonstrated Scotty's early renown. Though the newspaper rarely bothered with desert affairs other than economic developments, when prospectors found a body near isolated Saratoga Springs, it speculated that the murder victim might be Scott ("Cruel Desert's Victim Said to Be Scott"). It wasn't ("Murdered for Money in Lonely Spot"). However, the plot thickened, and missing Scott himself became a murder suspect ("Another Corpse Found in the Desert"). That this

and soft and did his traveling in an auto. Many tales have been told of him, but he was well liked by the desert dwellers. He never gave any of them cause for complaint.

In July of the year 1903, the San Pedro, Los Angeles & Salt Lake Railway began the construction of tracks from Daggett to Salt Lake City, Utah. Seymour Alf of Daggett received the first contract. He was the last of the twenty-mule teamers. He had long hauled borax from the Calicos to Daggett, but the building of a branch railway ended that. Now his teams were grading the roadbed. With the coming of cool weather more contractors strung camps over the desert, moving dirt with Fresno scrapers drawn by mules and horses. Two dollars a day for ten hours' work was the standard wage, though Alf paid more. Seventy-five cents a day for board, employment office dues, hospital fees, and other items reduced the net returns to less than one dollar a day.

Daggett had its birth in 1882 when a railway building eastward to meet the oncoming Santa Fe Railway established a station there because it was the nearest point to the booming mining town of Calico. It had never been deemed a tough town, although during its brief history there had been a few shooting scrapes, a couple of murders, and a lynching.* Occasionally, festive souls blowing a stake got rowdy

---

last piece refers to Scott as Albert rather than Walter possibly points to another man with the same last name, or it may reflect the scrambling of information by the time it arrived in Los Angeles from the far reaches of the desert. Given the dates of the articles and other circumstances surrounding the reputation of the mercurial Scotty, the references likely are to events related in this section.

*The lynching likely is the incident passed on by raconteur W. Storrs Lee. The loneliness, the long, unrelieved grind, and the hideous heat of desert trips often caused emotional pustules to break between drivers of twenty-mule teams and their swampers, or helpers, as they hauled borax across the desert. After recounting the story of a swamper who brained his partner with a shovel but got away with the murder because authorities had better things to do than investigate the site of a crime in the middle of nowhere, Lee tells a tale with a different ending: "Less fortunate was a fellow swamper who pursued his skinner to Daggett, seventy-five miles east of Mojave, cornered him behind a blacksmith shop, and pommeled the archenemy into pulp with a handy wheel spoke. The killer was quickly identified and locked up, and when it became evident that the justice was about to release him for the usual lack of evidence, a masked mob

and became a nuisance that perhaps needed abatement, but there was nothing new in that. Besides, the carousers added gaiety to the drab surroundings and circulated money. Many small towns were then partially supported by vice, which was condoned as a necessary evil.

Large numbers of men passed through the town on their way to work at the railway camps. Many returned with checks they cashed in Daggett saloons. Drunken laborers with money were easy pickings, and the town got bad. Gamblers, strumpets, pimps, and thieves descended upon it and made it a rendezvous. For a time, they did very much as they desired. They left the natives alone. It was not good policy to provoke hostilities with them. They were poor prey anyway. Many of them had guns and could shoot them. There was no profit in them.

Old Mike Walsh did not encourage the trade of the riffraff that invaded the town.

"That trade is too damned tough for me," he remarked.

Mike's elderly wife was reputed to have been a fillet de joy whom he had acquired informally, but that was a long time since, and it was not held against her. Mike allowed no women, negroes, and did not want Mexicans in his saloon. Alex's saloon was the favored rendezvous of the newcomers. It could hold one hundred men, and on cold winter nights it was often filled to capacity. Alex then did not dare attempt closing the place and turning them into the street.

One night a Mexican was shot and killed in Alex's. Fights were common there, but this was his first killing, although not the first attempt. When the coroner arrived and held the inquest, there was a dearth of witnesses, although the saloon had been crowded. Old Doc Pitman, the Coroner, was a jolly old soul who loved to visit a desert saloon and make merry with the boys. Now Old Doc became choleric and scolded and quizzed the witnesses in a vain effort to extort facts.

"Mister Coroner," testified one, "I was in such a hurry to get away, I niver had time to look back."

---

took charge. The prisoner was dragged from the security of the jail; a rope thrown over the crossarm of one of the new Santa Fe telegraph poles did the rest" (119).

The jury rendered a verdict of death by parties unknown, and that ended the matter. Nothing more was done except burying the Mexican on the hillside.

Thereafter, Alex's place became known as the Bucket of Blood and acquired a wide and unsavory notoriety. A traveling salesman desired to gratify his curiosity by inspecting the place. He gratified it, all right.

Walking boldly in and up to the bar, he laid down a half dollar and ordered a drink. A husky ruffian leaned over his shoulder and appropriated the half dollar. The victim started to leave but was stopped by another ruffian.

"Yez don't git out of here without setting up the drinks," he menacingly declared.

The salesman laid a $5 gold coin on the bar, and when the crowd lined up to drink, he bolted out the door and raced across the tracks into the railway depot. He remained there until a train took him away.

Old Bob, the Constable, was the only peace officer. It was not his duty to do police work, and he was too old and fond of whiskey, which he could get for nothing. Some of the townsmen wearied of conditions and complained to the Sheriff. Daggett was ninety miles from San Bernardino, the County Seat, and there was only one passenger train a day going either way. The Sheriff had but a few deputies, and the County authorities had always regarded the desert as a barbarous land whose primitive inhabitants could best settle their own troubles. When some ranchers living farther up the river complained about a local bully who terrorized his neighbors, the District Attorney growled,

"Don't you people know how to get rid of that fellow?"

They did.

One day his dead body, riddled with buckshot, was found in a neighbor's gateway. Only a perfunctory inquiry was made. No one could be found who knew anything.

Due to the urgings of a reform faction in Daggett, one day the Sheriff came with a deputy and arrested four pimps. One, a young mulatto, fled the town, running past the ranch. Dix saw him, and soon the Sheriff and Old Bob appeared driving a buggy. A few minutes later a deputy came on foot, and borrowing Dix's horse, soon captured the fugitive.

John Ralphs, the Sheriff, was the ideal picture of a frontier Sheriff. A big, brawny man, with a shaggy mane of black hair and big mustache, his very appearance and deep, loud voice was sufficient to intimidate most wrong-doers. Nor did he belie his looks. His reputation for fearlessness was not questioned. The deputy, compared with his chief, appeared small and frail and only fit to preside over a ladies' ribbon counter. Said Dix to Old Bob,

"That's a puny-looking deputy Ralphs packs around with him."

"Never you mind that feller's looks," retorted Bob. "Thet don't make them no better. He's got the nerve, and that's all it takes."

The deputy was W. S. McNabb. He studied law and later became United States District Attorney for Southern California.

The culprits were locked in the town jail. It is now preserved as a curiosity. One in a class by itself. Long before, it had been built by a local Constable and designed only to hold drunks and tramps. It was built of pine boards two by four inches thick. For the roof and floor they were laid edgeways, for the walls and door they were laid flatways. The boards were securely nailed together with long spikes. A long hasp spanned the door and was secured with a big padlock. Old Bob and the Sheriff guarded it during the night. The prisoners' lady friends, with whiskey and blandishments, persuaded a Mexican to attempt to break open the door. He soon found himself inside. Old Bob lay on the ground, fell asleep, rolled over, and his gun discharged. Nothing was hit and only Bob disturbed.

The next day the defendants demanded a jury trial. One debonair young scamp had been released upon depositing $50 bail. Now he appeared for trial, feeling sure of quick acquittal. No doubt, the Sheriff concurred in this belief and for this reason had released him on such a small amount. Who had ever heard of anyone in the desert being convicted of such a technical offense? It was a profession that had always existed on the frontier, and many deemed it a legitimate trade. The trial was sure to be a farce. No Daggett jury would convict. So said the wise ones. There were no lawyers to prolong the trial, and it was quickly over.

"Your Honor," reported the jury foreman, "we find the defendants guilty as charged."

The amazed spectators were hushed. Sternly decreed the Judge,

"It is the judgment of the court that each of you shall serve six months in the County Jail."

The stunned crowd silently filed out.

"I durn near fainted," said Old Bob.

"The Judge has sure got plenty of guts," remarked Old Mike.

The decent people in the town were jubilant and loud in their praises of the Judge. The complaints of others were unprintable.

When the railway construction began, the impression prevailed that Daggett would become an important town.* The town had a young doctor. Lured by false hopes, an elderly one arrived and opened an office. He wore a long-tailed, black coat and a wise, benign look, but he soon starved out.

A deluded, old couple came laden with provisions and equipment for a bakery. They lingered for a few days and dolefully sold their chattels and departed. A Mexican thrived with a lunch wagon patronized by the nighthawks. Excepting some brothels, this was the only new business establishment.

There was one firm of Swede contractors who usually operated a saloon where their employees would be fleeced of their earnings. Evil tales were told of men who labored long without drawing pay, being enticed into getting drunk, and on the following day being informed they were in debt to the contractors. The Swedes leased for one year a building from Old Mike. After paying one month's rent, they learned to their consternation that the County Supervisors deemed three saloons enough for Daggett and would license no more.

---

*It did not. Still told with a wry grin around Daggett, the story goes that when rumors flew that the railroad planned to expand facilities in the town, happy locals swiftly raised the price of their real estate. In reaction, the railroad moved a few miles up the road, built extensive repair yards in Barstow—and once more Daggett missed the brass ring.

When the rent became in arrears, Mike filed a suit and sent the Constable to the construction camp to levy a writ of attachment upon the mules. They tried to compromise and surrender the lease. Mike refused. Said he,

"Some of you fellers might get caught in town some night and need a place to sleep, then that place will come in handy. Keep it. You may need it. And don't forgit to send the rent every month. If you do, I'll send that Constable agin."

Mike told this with gusto.

"Those damned Swedes would stick it in me quick enough if they had a chance," he chuckled.

A young Chinese restaurateur went to Stockton and bought a young wife for $400. Being a canny Chink, he refused to abide by ancient Chinese customs and refused to buy sight unseen. The matter was settled without outraging social proprieties by the father hiding the buyer and sending the girl into the yard to catch a chicken.

He saw. He bought. He got a bargain. She learned English and developed into a very competent businesswoman.

The local butcher garnered wealth that he later lost in foolish investments. There was no regular schedule for the construction train. Imported meats often spoiled in the Daggett depot. The butcher could deliver freshly killed beef whenever the train left Daggett.

The town's evil reputation spread. The Judge had for many years been a contributor to the *Los Angeles Times*. The paper requested him to send them a description of Daggett. He declined. They sent a young reporter, Harry Carr. He afterwards became a famous writer. Mr. Carr's recital was spread over several papers in three consecutive issues of the *Times*. He drew a very lurid picture.*

*Harry Carr's fine, sardonic eye creates sensational desert vignettes, of thugs invading towns and enterprising "ladies of small virtue" offering their services in the tents of ephemeral frontier settlements. Carr devotes "Wolves on Desert," the second of his three-part series on the coming of the railroad to the Mojave, to the evils of Daggett. The piece begins: "A high carnival of crime has started in this town." Lacking a by-line, "M'Kinney Dies Fighting Officers at Bakersfield," along with similar articles in the *Times* of this general period, shows how Angelenos liked to be dazzled by garish events in the rural expanses they referred to as the "cow counties."

9 SHIVAREES ◆ A LAWMAN DANDY ◆ THE JUDGE BECOMES AN ARTIST ◆ Whatever Daggett's evil repute, the permanent inhabitants went about their business as usual. Children went to school and attended Sunday school. Occasionally, a preacher came and harangued the few people at his meetings in the schoolhouse. Public dances continued. At times, a group of young folks would enjoy a hayride. With a four-horse team and a hay wagon, Dix would take them to the canal heading, where a large fire was built and a tasty meal consumed. Everything was home-cooked by the ladies. No lunch stuff was bought from the stores, nor was liquor taken. These were decorous affairs but much enjoyed.

At long intervals there was a marriage. Old custom made it incumbent on the groom to buy drinks for his friends. The kids usually shivareed the couple until the groom bought peace with a liberal dispensation of candy. One couple who had disdained these social amenities was treated each night to explosions of dynamite close enough to shake their house. After three nights, the besiegers gave up. If, however, the newlyweds were not liked, they were just ignored and no notice taken of them.

The year before, two well-drillers had visited the ranch, and this year they returned and seemed pleased with the results. In November they returned with thirty farmers from the Coast whom they had enticed with glowing descriptions of fine government land to be had for nothing. They arrived in the night, hired all the local rigs, and passed the ranch before dawn. The farmers spent the day inspecting several miles easterly and returned too mad and disgusted to stop at the ranch. They left that night after vowing they would try to get the name Daggett changed to Dammit.

The Judge wrote to Dieterle:

> You may spare yourself further mentioning of town lots or railroads in your letters. We are not going to crawl out on either. Daggett may have 500 people in the next two or three years, but as yet the only gain is in hoboes and bums, and no one dreams of enquiring about lots. Three new shanties and fixing up the old stone building constitute the improvements so far.

He was still mad and disgusted with his failures but determined to remain and fight it out. Dix was more cheerful:

"What difference does it make?" he declared. "If I was working for wages I would not have anything anyway."

To protect their property, the Santa Fe Railway Company sent a special officer at their own expense to live in Daggett. Billy Smithson was only twenty-four years old and had never before worn a star. He afterwards related that before coming he had been warned to go well armed at all times and to take no chances. When he arrived at 2 A.M., he tried to enter the railway depot but found the floor of the waiting room packed solid with sleeping bums. It always was on a cold night. Recoiling in disgust, he crossed the street to Alex's saloon. This was filled with a barbarous-looking crowd. Many drunk and some quarreling and fighting. It required all the courage he could muster to refrain from returning on the next train.

Billy wore good clothes. Perhaps he did so to please his attractive young wife. For two weeks he strolled leisurely about with his high, stiff, white collar and ties, seeming to be a young dandy striving to impress feminine hearts. He was an amiable, harmless young man anxious to please, and he offended no one. People liked him, but his foppish clothes were by some regarded as indicating weakness of character. The desert rat rarely dressed up except for special occasions, like a dance.

One day with Old Bob trailing behind, he strolled down the street delivering a verbal ultimatum. Those without lawful business in Daggett must leave. No longer would it be a home for undesirable elements. Little heed was given. Who was this young squirt who thought he could run the town? He had better return whence he came before someone busted him in two. Did it not beat all how wearing a star could swell some guy's head?

Now, neither officer was ever seen without a cane made from a shortened billiard cue and a cartridge belt with a revolver in an open holster. Billy carried his gun in front, the holster supported by his left suspender.

"Someday," he said, "I may have to grab that quick."

Three years later he failed to do so quickly enough.

Billy began arresting the loafers and taking them before the Judge, who on vagrancy charges sentenced them to terms in the County Jail. The few arrests started a migration. Thereafter, roughs and criminals passed through but did not linger.

It required courage for the Judge, an old man living in an isolated shack a mile from town and often alone, to fearlessly impose jail sentences. A visiting brother from New Jersey solicitously enquired,

"Theo, are you not afraid that some of these toughs you send to jail will seek revenge upon you?"

He replied: "Whenever a man gets to thinking of things like that, it is time to quit being Judge."

Nothing ever daunted him from doing what he believed to be his duty, and he enjoined his son always to perform what he termed "obligations of honor" and never to make promises unless he believed he could fulfill them.

Long ago during the Miocene Age, the Mojave River was a great stream that formed a large lake in the eastern part of the Silver Valley. The thick beds of lacustrine clay that are now exposed show that the lake lasted over a long period. On them scientists have gathered the bones of long-extinct animals. In time, some cataclysm of nature enabled the water to burst through the encircling hills and pour into the deep rift in the earth's crust, of which Death Valley forms a portion. In ten miles the river dropped 1,000 feet. This caused it to cut backward and scour a deep, wide groove through the valley's floor. In time, the increasing aridity of the climate ended this. Now the grade of the river increases as one goes downstream, which is the reverse of most rivers.

Twenty miles below Daggett, the river flows through a mile-wide trough seventy feet below the valley floor. Six miles of this is well watered by the subsurface waters of the river and by springs flowing in from the sides. Much of it was covered with groves of mesquite, willow, and cottonwood, some with grassy meadows. On the adjacent valley are wide areas of bunch grass, both galleta and sand grass. The former grows in warm weather, the latter in cool weather. The mesquites produce heavy crops of nutritious beans that are greedily eaten by livestock.

This was long a rendezvous and recruiting ground for the Spanish caravans bound for New Mexico in springtime with great herds of livestock. Later, it was a haven for the emigrants crossing the desert, who lingered here to recuperate their worn stock. Because of hostile Indians, the government long maintained a military post there and made a military reservation of the timbered bottomlands. All this was in the past. Now four squatters occupied different portions, ran small herds of stock, and jealously regarded each other's occupancy. There was plenty of quail, doves, ducks, and rabbits to eke out a meager living. Visitors seldom came, and it was a fine location for one contented with an isolated life.

An old gentleman named Mudgett with an elderly nephew occupied the upper end of the timber. They were survivors of the old race of hunters and trappers. Bill Frakes, the nephew, irked by crowding civilization, had emigrated to Argentina, spent ten years on the frontier of that country, and had recently returned. Now he was engaged in trapping the wild desert sheep and making futile endeavors to cross them with domestic sheep and secure a hardy breed.

Mr. Mudgett occasionally came to Daggett carrying in his hind pocket a small cap-and-ball revolver.

"Mr. Mudgett," inquired Dix, "why do you carry that pistol?"

"Well, Suh, if a man don't tote a gun all the time, he moughten to have it when he wants it," he replied.

Dix and the owner of several horses hauled a winter's supply of firewood from near Mudgett's home. Frakes, learning that the Judge was an old hunter and writer of hunting lore, called on him. After discussing many things, Frakes inquired,

"Mr. Van Dyke, did you ever hear a mountain lion scream?"

"No, and I don't believe anyone else ever did," the Judge replied.

"Well, I never did," rejoined Frakes, "and I have often wondered whether anyone else ever had."

The local cobbler, a French Canadian from a land where buckwheat thrived, made futile efforts to persuade the Judge to grow it:

"All doz tings in the ground dat are bad, the buckwheat take him out," he declaimed.

"Maybe," said the Judge.

He later said to Dix: "These fellows are right about the land having pizen in it, even if alkali don't show on the surface. If there is, we should be able to leach it out of this porous soil. We will try it and see what results we get."

They diked four acres with dirt ridges and kept them filled with water until the Judge estimated that twenty feet in depth had filtered through the soil.

"If there is any pizen, that should take it out," he declared.

Later, they were to learn that their sole achievement had been to leach out most of the soluble fertility in the soil.

During a long period the Judge had contributed hunting articles to eastern magazines. The ludicrous attempts of eastern artists to depict California hunting scenes had caused him much agony. Late in life he wrote an editor a critical letter. Being unable to express his ideas in polite language, he supplemented them with crude pencil sketches to furnish an idea of what a hunting picture should depict. It probably made little impression on the editor, but the Judge conceived the idea that he could learn to properly illustrate his own writings. It seemed ridiculous for an old man to attempt unaided to become an artist, but persevering labor brought results, and in time many of his pictures were published.*

The Judge had inherited a natural sense and love of beauty, and he knew colors. Long before, his descriptive writings of nature's beauty had resulted in his being renowned as "The Word Painter." Now, during his periods of relaxation, he often gazed at the mountains that enclosed the valley. Like a spectroscope, the dry desert air splits the

---

*A sampling of Theodore's accurate drawings in this mode may be seen in his *The Still-Hunter*. Here, the purpose of the sketches is instructive, to illustrate the fine points of hunting discussed in the text; they should not be confused with the several artistic pieces by Carl Rungius, one of the finest wildlife painters of the day, which Theodore included in his book.

sun's rays into the varied colors that compose them. These the barren rocks reflect in shades and tints that constantly change with the passage of the sun. The varying, brilliant colors of the desert landscape, the deep blue shadows in the canyons, and the bright sky colors composed of many hues charmed and fascinated him. No artist has ever been able to reproduce these colors, but the Judge found much pleasure in trying. Hereafter, he spent much of his leisure mixing brilliant watercolor pigments and attempting to portray the marvelous colors. Perseverance made him quite proficient, and some admirers paid real money to secure them.*

The farmers began the new year of 1904 with cheerful spirits. There was no flood in the river, but there was sufficient water. The season was favorable, and there were no destructive winds. Once more the garden truck was planted and coddled and cared for.

"Now," the Judge hopefully announced, "we will show that the land is good for something."

But the crops were poorer than ever, and the poorest was upon the leached land. The Judge salvaged for a curiosity a two-foot corn stalk bearing a matured nubbin.

The Judge was a well-bred gentleman and a fine English scholar. Once, when asked by his son whether he ever used a dictionary, he replied,

"No. Whenever a man of my education has to seek the meaning of a word, he should not use it."

He had even written an elementary grammar that was never published. Before coming to the desert, he had rarely spoken a profane word. Two years of blasted hopes and a diet of canned vegetables made him proficient. He found his book English inadequate to express his opinions of the tribulations and disappointments he endured.

With the coming of summer, his vituperative remarks ceased. He no longer fumed and fretted. The alfalfa was now making a rank growth of leafy, fine-stemmed plants, and the villagers were coming

---

*The archives of Barstow's Mojave River Valley Museum contain two untitled, undated, but skillfully done watercolors of desert mountains signed by Theodore. See the "Paintings" entry for Theodore in the Select Bibliography.

and gazing at the field in amazement. Even the stunted yellow plants that last year appeared so hopeless and forlorn were now racing to catch up with the others. Alfalfa is a deep-rooted perennial, and it was very evident that with another year's growth the plants would be deeper rooted and yield much heavier crops. Now the Judge greeted visitors with cheerful smiles and gladly showed them over the hay field while he bragged about it and made glowing prophecies of the things he would achieve.

To his son he chortled, "We will show that damned gang yet that we can make a farm out of this."

Mr. H. W. Keller, a prominent citizen of Los Angeles, came for a visit. He and the Judge had often gone together on hunting trips. He enjoyed himself immensely and had great sport shooting doves, which were very numerous.

On his return home he related his experiences with much relish.

"I asked Van Dyke if Daggett was not a tough town. He said no. I told him it was the toughest-looking place I had ever been in. He insisted that it was a quiet, peaceful town. The night I left he escorted me to the railway depot with a double-barreled shotgun."

Daggett did seem tame to those who had resided there before the coming of Billy Smithson. Billy continued to wear his stiff, white collar until hot weather came and wilted it. Then he gave up.

The new railway started a new town four miles from Daggett. It was named Otis in honor of General Otis, the owner of the *Los Angeles Times*. It was a dubious honor. A traveling Socialist organizer later described it in a Socialist paper as being "a fine example of the Capitalistic system. The town consisted of a lot of tents and shacks, and the only respectable-looking house in the town is a house of prostitution."

10 SLICK TRICKS ♦ THE JUDGE HOLDS COURT ♦ OLD FISHER BLOWN UP ♦ THE LAST INDIANS ♦ A restaurant keeper boldly sold liquor without a license. This intercepted some of the Daggett liquor trade. Old Mike did not care, but the owners of the other two saloons became wrought up over it. They proclaimed that they paid license fees and deserved protection for their businesses. The only time they ever observed liquor laws was on election days. Then the front door was closed, and patrons had to enter by the rear door. They secured the restaurant keeper's arrest. He pleaded guilty. The Judge knew what instigated his arrest. He fined him $10 but enjoined him to sin no more. The judgment brought wails of anguish from the prosecutors and caused a visiting preacher to call upon the Judge to ascertain whether he was a lost soul. The townsmen were pleased. Most of them were tired of the prosecutors running their own saloons without regard for law or public decency. The resentment was later to develop into active hostility.

The summer waned. The farmers being cheered by the sale of $300 worth of hay that brought a good price. The borax mill continued to pay $75 a month for water. The mill dug two wells but could not pump enough water from them.

Seven miles away, the bed of an ancient Miocene lake lay buried beneath the valley floor. It contained 5 percent borax and was too hard to dissolve in water. It was mined like rock ore, hauled on a narrow-gauge railway to the mill, put in wooden tanks, filled with water, and crushed by heavy stone wheels rolling around inside the tank. Sulphur brought in straw sacks from Japan was cooked in great retorts and the fumes forced through the mud soup. After the mud settled, the liquor was drawn off into several acres of vats two feet deep and left for the sun and wind to evaporate. The residue was almost pure boric acid. The mud remaining was sluiced into the adjacent riverbottom. The evaporation sometimes equaled one inch a day. Sometimes wild fowl would light on the ponds and either sicken from drinking the water or get their wings encrusted with the borax. The crude acid was sacked and shipped east to be refined.

This plant belonged to the American Borax Company, which was owned by the Standard Sanitary Ware Company. They used the output for enameling porcelain plumbing. They were trying to supply their own needs at less cost than they could buy the material. Henry Blumenberg, the manager, was eager to secure a richer borax deposit. The mill employed two chemists and assayers, and Henry spread the news that they would gladly assay free of cost anything prospectors brought in. The Pacific Coast Borax Company was shipping rich borax ore by rail to a refinery on the Coast, and this enabled a clever miner who was broke and wished to return to his home in New Mexico to do so at Henry's expense.

One day he appeared at the mill with several ore specimens and requested a free assay. He had included a sample of borax ore. When he returned, no mention of borax was made to him. The superintendent, Mr. Bouldin, was quite assiduous in his attentions and intimated that Mr. Blumenberg might be interested in one of his claims that seemed a promising copper prospect. Pete Le Sarge was a French peasant boy who had deserted from the army of France and fled to America. For many years he had roamed the desert working in mines and prospecting. He had never lost the French thrift learned in his youth. Pete always had plenty of money. In 1914, he gathered a party of young Frenchmen and returned to fight for his native land. Pete paid the traveling expenses of the group. Five years later, he returned.

"They only allowed me to fight two years," he said. "They told me I was too old and sent me home to work on the farm."

Pete was a freelance miner operating on his own. When he saw Mr. Bouldin and a stranger board the railway train and learned their destination, he became suspicious. He knew that a tip about a new borax discovery was probably the lure. He boarded the next train for the same place.

Mr. Jack Duane was a commission merchant who dealt in mining supplies and was on cordial terms with the staff of the Pacific Borax Company. His office was in the railway depot, and he observed the departure of the three. He telegraphed Wash Cahill, one of the staff stationed at Ludlow farther east, that something was in the wind and should be investigated. Mr. Cahill boarded the next train for the same destination. On arriving there, he located Pete, said they were both on the same mission, and proposed a joining of interests. Pete declined. He had little faith in corporations or their representatives.

Mr. Bouldin hired a livery team and was guided to some claims several miles away. After a careful investigation that revealed no evidence of borax formations, he asked the miner where he had gotten his sample of borax.

"I never had any borax. I don't even know what it looks like," he replied.

Mr. Bouldin described its appearance. The miner feigned amazement.

"Why, I did pick up a chunk of white stuff where they were loading cars, but I did not know what it was. I did not know I got it mixed with those ore samples I took to the mill."

Henry prided himself on being clever, and he did not relish the jokes and laughter of the townsmen. His was some consolation to the other victims.

An even slicker trick was played by a prospector who found some talc, which closely resembles borax ore. He dug a pit, hauled away the material he took out, then secured a wagonload of borax ore and dumped that beside the hole. He beguiled a confiding investor into paying $1,200 for a half interest. Two weeks later he endeavored to sell the remainder. This aroused the sucker's suspicions. He secured a team and returned for further investigations, but when he returned, the swindler had fled.

On the north side of the ranch shack, there was a rude veranda. The floor was dirt and the roof rough boards that shed little rain. It was the only shady spot, and here in summer the Judge informally held court. There was always a heap of melons beside the house, and the Judge would always open court by cutting melons and distributing large chunks to everyone. When this was done with Mexicans, it exasperated the Constable.

"Why don't he send them damned greasers to jail instead of feeding them melons and turning them loose?" he complained to his cronies.

But the Judge was a tolerant soul. He had traveled much in Old Mexico and knew these poor immigrants to be simple, primitive folk, toiling in a strange land for a beggarly wage. They could neither read or write any language or speak English. Why should they be expected to understand American laws and customs? Why send them to jail for trivial offenses that perhaps had been done through ignorance? They had harmed no one. Why expect as much from them as those who were born to the soil and should know better? After conversing kindly with them in Spanish, and gently admonishing them, he usually dismissed them.

By now the Judge was renowned over the desert for legal knowledge and for his willingness to listen patiently to people's troubles and to give sound advice. All kinds came. Even the soiled doves and other outcasts confided their troubles and received kindly consideration. At times it was embarrassing when both litigants privately related their troubles and asked advice, after which the Judge had to hold trial and pass judgment. This was contrary both to law and judicial ethics, but he ignored them. There was no lawyer within ninety miles. How could he dispense justice to bewildered ones who did not know their rights or how to protect them? Laws were complicated things. They were only rules, and few of them were needed for these primitive conditions.

Trials were held with little formality, except on rare occasions when an imported lawyer tried to presume upon what he deemed an ignorant backwoods judge. Jury trials were held in Mike's dancehall beside the saloon. On such occasions, the Judge was the only one who felt obliged to refrain from refreshments. He would drink nothing until court proceedings were ended. This had been his rule when pleading cases in court for others.

Mike never drank. Leastways no one ever saw him do so. When a bar patron sociably invited him to join in a drink, Mike took a fifteen-cent cigar from its box, stuck it in his vest pocket, and returned it after the customer had departed. Mike loaned the dancehall to anyone who desired to promote a dance. The bar patronage satisfied him. For one dance the colored barber was engaged to fiddle. This angered Mike:

"I don't mind cleaning that hall out for a white man," he complained, "but I'll be damned if I want to do it for a naygur."

Ginger Smith, the post office clerk, sympathized with Mike. Ginger was a new arrival from Missouri and could not become reconciled to the local tolerance shown the few colored people in the town. It caused Ginger more than mental distress, because he would not enter the Chink restaurant without first peering in. If he saw a darky, he would go hungry rather than eat in the same room. Part of the time he clerked in the adjoining grocery store, and it galled his haughty spirit to be compelled to wait on colored patrons. One day Dix increased his misery by throwing a big, harmless gopher snake into the store. Ginger fled, and the snake found refuge in the cellar, where surplus stock was stored. Thereafter, Ginger was afraid to go into the cellar.

"This ain't Missouri. What do you expect those coons to do, go hungry?" queried Old Davis, who lived down the river in a rude cabin built of poles and dieted on wild game and mesquite beans.

"He's another nigger lover," sniffed Ginger after the old man had left.

"When you eat with negroes, you make social equals of them," ponderously proclaimed the schoolteacher. He was a Pennsylvania Dutchman devoid of a sense of humor and stooped from carrying an overload of personal dignity. One night returning from a hayride, he and a lady visitor sat on the rear end of the hay rack, conversing in German. A cool wind was blowing, and he gallantly shielded her with a piece of canvas. The next day Dix encountered him while in a great rage. His eyes were sticking out, and he raved incoherently. Some wag had informed him that the news was all over town that he had been furtively kissing the lady beneath the shelter of the canvas.

"That is the last social function I will ever attend in Daggett," he sputtered.

Dix failed to convince him that he was being kidded, and he continued to air his grievance until the whole town was laughing at him.

The remnants of Old Fisher, an eccentric German, were found in a mine tunnel where he had been working alone. Dynamite had blown him to pieces.

"That crazy Dutchman blew himself up on purpose," declared Mr. Garinger.

"I seen him take an auger and bore down a hole that had misfired and pull out the dynamite cap. I quit working with him right there."

Those who knew Fisher concurred. He had.

A few remnants of the once numerous Paiute Indians yet roamed the desert. They no longer lived a savage life. They had horses, wagons, guns, store clothes, and a hankering for white man's grub. They were industrious and thrifty and occasionally worked at various jobs. They did not need much to gratify their simple wants. The Newberry Mountains lay ten miles east of the ranch. Sheep thrived on the rugged heights, and on each side of the mountains were springs where they drank in hot weather. Here the Indian hunters would patiently lie in wait for them.

11 MORE ABOUT INDIANS ♦ SPIRITUALISTS ♦ DISASTERS WITH WATER AND BOOZE ♦ A MAN TIED TO A TREE ♦ Where a point of the mountains extended into the valley, there was a tract of damp land where grass, wild grapes, and mesquite trees flourished. In summer it was a favored resort of a small band of Paiute Indians who eked out a meager living with mesquite beans and wild game. They brought to the ranch fine dressed sheep hides that, when cut in strips, wet and rolled in the hands, and then dried, made the toughest and strongest of thongs.*

The squaws first scraped off all the hair and meat and smoked the hides. Then they were made soft and pliable by rubbing and kneading between the hands. The farmers bought a dozen for $2 each, and the Indians gladly assisted in harvesting the hay. Their earnings were invested in food and merchandise with which they returned to their camp. A passing prospector gave one too much whiskey, from which he died. The next day, the victim was buried, and all his personal belongings were burned. The Indians believed this would ensure their transportation to the same destination as the deceased was due to arrive at. This was the last of the old Indian hunters. The next genera-

---

*Dix's nephew, Alan Golden, pointed out an area on the southwest corner of the ranch that his mother, Mary Van Dyke Golden, called the Indian Camp. Dix's sister, she could remember Indians camping there when she was a child. In another link to the past, Mr. Golden also showed me a pair of moccasins and a tanned bighorn-sheep skin apparently traded from the Paiutes. Amazingly, after all these years the skin was the softest I've ever seen, almost nubilous.

tion gravitated to the white settlements where they could slave and earn enough to possess autos and other newfangled contraptions their fathers had never dreamed of.

The year 1904 was dry. It was the last of a series of eleven dry years. A cycle of twelve wet years followed. It was dry both in California and Arizona. For eight months no rain fell in Arizona, and as summer waned, despair began to settle on the land. In August the drought ended with a deluge in many places. For several days at a stretch no through trains passed Daggett. Temporary bridge repairs were soon wrecked by fresh torrents.

At the canal heading an insignificant gully entered. It appeared so trivial that it had never occurred to anyone to make a shortcut and empty it into the river above. Now a torrent scoured it wide and deep and deposited the debris in the canal. It had been fifteen feet deeper than the river; now at the head the bottom was five feet higher. For a thousand feet the great canal was partially filled.

With gloomy forebodings Dix surveyed the ruin. No water would now flow, and they possessed neither money nor equipment to remove the debris. It looked like this was the end. As he rode homeward, Dix whistled and made futile efforts to feel cheerful. He was still very young and had worked hard to establish a home. He wondered if this calamity would end it all and send him forth seeking a job from others.

The Judge was not troubled.

"Shucks," he replied to Dix's lugubrious revelations. "That ain't nothing. I could not ask anyone to invest money here until I knew the land would grow alfalfa. Now I can tell them it will. I have been wanting a concrete pipe in that blasted ditch. Now we will get one."

Undaunted, the Judge departed for Los Angeles. His optimism cheered Dix. He had faith in his father and felt that all was well. The Judge soon returned with smiles and a contractor to bid on the work. Preparations were begun for the construction and the laying of one mile of thirty-inch concrete pipe.

Arthur Bent of Los Angeles was the contractor, and he sent fifteen husky Slavonians to do the work. The concrete was mixed by hand with hoes, tamped by hand into molds, which were immediately removed and the two-foot joint of pipe left standing on end. A tank twenty-five feet high was erected, and two men kept the green pipe sprinkled with water for ten days. This was done to cure it slowly. If it dried too quickly, it would crumble. It had to be good pipe to stand handling. The men were paid $2.50 a day, lived in tents, and cooked their own food.

Dix had to haul cement, gravel, and pipe. He had to dig the ditch and distribute the pipe along it. The pipe was laid in a sub ditch dug three feet deep in the floor of the large canal. Three tents were erected for Dix's crew, one to cook and eat in, and the others for sleeping. The beds were laid on the ground with hay for mattresses. Everything was crude and primitive, but his men were contented. Dix picked them off the railway track while they were hoboing to some vague destination. It was cold weather, and the wages of $1.25 a day and board for ten hours' work was better than the railway contractors paid. They worked hard. Even so, they were no match for the Hunkies. At times when a shortage of cement ended pipe-making temporarily, and Dix hired the concrete men to dig ditch, they dug twice the amount his hobo gang did. If a cook quit, there was always a shoveler eager for the job and claiming to be a cook. They did not have to know much to cook a satisfactory meal. Fancy vittles for laborers had not yet become an established custom.

The miles of pipe was made, and all but 500 feet laid and covered. Lack of funds caused a suspension of work.

There were three associates. William Dieterle and William G. Kerckhoff were businessmen of Los Angeles. They were victims of the old canal company anxious to recuperate their losses. The third, Dr. A. R. Rhea, had been a pioneer doctor in Calico and Daggett. Like others, he had dabbled in mines and three years before had been lucky enough to sell some mining claims for $35,000 cash. Some years before, tiring of bachelorhood, he brought from the East an old maid he had known in his youth. She was a thrifty wife and a shrewd trader. He gave her a small portion of the money from the sale, which careful manipulating increased. In her old age she possessed $80,000, which two slick oil-stock salesmen swindled her of. But that is another story.

Dr. Rhea had been one of the original incorporators of the first company and had furnished money to begin the ranch. He and Kerckhoff had agreed to furnish the funds to pay for the pipe. Rhea's intentions were good, but like many who have been lucky enough to gain sudden wealth, he was an incurable optimist. He also had an unfortunate habit of consulting spiritualist mediums about investments. He was a firm believer in spiritualism. His wife was a devout church member, but each respected the other's belief, and they refrained from quarrels.

Rhea invested all of his money in a mine in the Panamint Mountains far out in the desert. He was so sure of future riches that he induced various of his friends to invest. He trusted the optimistic report of a person he had sent to investigate the mine. Now he learned too late that the mine was worthless. The whole investment was a total loss.

Kerckhoff was a wealthy man who did business on honorable but strict principles. When he learned that no one else was furnishing funds, he refused to do so. The farmers had the pleasant task of placating local debtors whom they were unable to pay. However, the pipe was laid. A winter flood came down the river and flowed long enough to raise the water levels, and sufficient irrigating water again reached the ranch.

At the November election, some of the Daggett residents were jolted out of a complacent existence by what was to some a calamity. Judge West had long been the County Supervisor. He was a crafty politician and had the support of the liquor interests. Candidates for office were then nominated by County Conventions. West was a Democrat and secured the nomination of that party. The Republican Convention failed to nominate a candidate. When the news reached Daggett, a gang of disgruntled voters made unavailing efforts to get Judge Van Dyke nominated by the Republican party. They cursed and damned politicians and wracked their wits with futile schemes to beat West.

It was customary for the County Clerk to send each voter a sample ballot a few days before election. This was to enable voters to decide how to mark their ballots before election day. At the bottom of the ticket was one line: "For granting liquor licenses. Yes - No."

There was no explanation, and the issue attracted no attention. The local medico, Dr. Mc Farlane, did not like the taste of liquor, did not like West, who was reputed to be an old soak, and did not like the saloons or their owners. He was regarded as an obstreperous young squirt, only twenty-five years old, who shot off his mouth too much, but he enjoyed doing it. In some way he learned that a local option law had been passed by the state legislature and that a No vote would forbid the issuing of liquor licenses in Daggett for two years and until the vote was reversed at some future election thereafter. Mc Farlane confided in a few trusted friends, and when the votes were counted, there were twenty-one No and eighteen Yes. Not a liquor dealer or his employees voted either way. They were in total ignorance of the matter. Less than half the voters voted either way.

Old Mike still operated a livery stable. On election night, he drove some voters back to the borax mine. He returned after the votes had been counted, and a snickering group was gathered in front of his saloon.

"It's all off with you, Mike," yelled the Doctor. "We have voted the town dry, and you will have to shut up."

"Old West will fix that for us," gleefully chortled Mike.

This brought some unprintable remarks from the Doctor, but Mike laughed heartily. He could not read and knew little law. He knew what a borax check should look like and could read figures. Other checks he refused to cash.

The next day a jovial crowd of wets laughed and joked about the election, and they did the same the following day. The idea of Daggett existing without saloons was something they could not conceive of. It was just as silly as dispensing with domestic water. They had always had booze. It could not be dispensed with. The third day they were a glum crowd. It was plain that word had come from the County Seat informing them that liquor licenses could not be renewed. They appealed to West, who had been reelected. He gave them no comfort.

"Why weren't you looking out for yourselves?" he chided. "There is nothing I can do for you."

It had not been a moral wave. Most of the rebels had been and were drinking men. Some even got drunk on occasion. Most of them denied voting on the question. Dix, being young and brash, freely asserted that he had voted dry. He did not like a wide-open town. Some three months later when meditating on the election, he recalled that in his ignorance he had inadvertently voted Yes instead of No. He concealed this information, believing that he was voting for the enactment of some restraining law. He never told anybody of his mistake.

One of the squatters at Camp Cady was an eccentric old German named Swanze, who had been a soldier at the Fort. He was an incurable kleptomaniac who stole things of no use to him and was regarded as being senile. On his infrequent trips to Daggett he was the butt of jokers. One night a hilarious crowd tied him to a tree and at intervals carried beer to him. But his guileless demeanor masked a fertile, cunning mind.

Marcus Pluth was a successful miner and prospector who had the rare faculty of correctly appraising the value of a prospective mine. He had made considerable money and was wise to all the tricks used in beguiling money from confiding investors. One day, Old Swanze appeared in town and informed Pluth that he had some samples of iron ore he desired his opinion of. Pluth knew all about the iron. It had no commercial value, but being a kindly, generous person, he condescended to look at it. Among the samples of iron Swanze had placed a small piece of rich copper ore. Pluth immediately spotted it.

12

CON GAMES ♦ ADVICE ON MATRIMONY AND TWO OR THREE DEAD MEN ♦ THE EUCALYPTUS BOOM ♦ BERT'S MURDER STORY

"Where did you get that?" he inquired.

"I don't know vat dot green stuff is. Dere vas only a couple uf feet uf dot," he replied. "But dot iron vas one hundred feet wide."

Ignoring the copper sample, he continued to talk volubly of the iron.

Pluth surreptitiously filched the copper specimen and sneaked off to where a close examination with a microscope revealed it to be rich in copper.

Mr. Swanze enjoyed a pleasant evening plied with good cigars and whiskey furnished by Pluth. He was charmed by the affability and courteous attentions of his host and allowed himself to be beguiled into extending him an invitation to return with him and personally inspect the iron deposit.

The next morning Swanze gloomily told Pluth his expected pension check had failed to arrive in the mail, and he would like to borrow $30 to buy grub. The loan was granted with such alacrity that Swanze bitterly repented not asking for more. The two left town together. Mr. Swanze had a fifteen-cent cigar between his teeth and lovingly clasped a bottle of Old Crow whiskey while Pluth drove his team. The loafers in front of Old Mike's watched them leave and indulged in idle speculation, wondering what kind of game Pluth was up to. Three days after vainly seeking a copper vein, Pluth returned mad and disgusted and hastened to Mike's to get a drink.

"If I was not a good-natured man," he declared, "I would have killed that damned lying Dutchman."

A dead man was found on the edge of the ranch beside the irrigating ditch. He lay on his face and had been dead about two weeks. The weather was cool and windy, and he had dried up. Many had passed by and deemed him asleep. Sleepers were a common sight. The body gave forth no odor, but the face turning black attracted attention. Another corpse was found along the new railway. Both legs had been cut off by a train. A revolver was clasped in the dead hand, and there was a bullet in his brain. It was surmised that while beating his way he had fallen beneath a train's wheels and had then committed suicide.

The railway company paid laborers in checks payable in Los Angeles and refused to allow them to ride a train unless they paid cash fare, which few could do. One unfortunately died of thirst within ten miles of Otis. Some Mexicans, themselves in dire straits for water, arrived in Otis and reported the man's sufferings, but rescuers found him dead.

The railway gave fare from Los Angeles to the job. This enabled some of the Daggett residents to save train fare. In the city they would give an employment agent a dollar for a job, get a pass, and leave the train at Daggett. A guard was usually sent to prevent desertions, but he could not restrain anyone. Nor could one be prosecuted for fraud unless it was proven that he had no intention of working when he was first engaged.

The Judge was still determined to grow garden truck. He detested canned grub. The stores imported vegetables by express train twice each week. The Los Angeles commission men sent what they could not sell there, and the stores only imported what could be immediately sold. Customers who came late secured only what others had disdained. There was no refrigeration system except an outdoor pantry, a wooden frame covered with burlap and kept wet with water. In hot weather, bacon, cheese, butter, eggs, and everything else that could dry out or melt down was kept in it. It was a poor resource, but there was nothing else but the "desert cooler," as it was called. In humid air it would have been worthless, but the dry desert air evaporated water rapidly enough to keep the inside cool. The hotter the weather, the greater was the evaporation.

The farmers secured bulletins from the University of Arizona telling what plants could thrive and bear crops in the hot, arid air of the desert, and some of the past mistakes could now be avoided.

"The trouble with that soil is poverty," declared the Judge. "What it needs is more fertility."

This seemed easy to remedy. Fertilizer had been accumulating in Daggett corrals for more than twenty years. In the desert it dried out and troubled no one any more than so much sawdust. Four acres were covered about four inches deep with manure and plowed under. One could expect that heat generated would injure crops in spots, but most of the fertilizer appeared to be thoroughly decayed. It was not. Again the garden failed. Melons and corn survived in places, but over most of the garden ground the heat generated by the decaying manure burned the vegetables. It had never rotted during the long years it lay in the open and now did so when plowed under and kept wet.

The Judge was mad and disgusted, but the alfalfa crops were consoling. The production increased so much that a baler was purchased to bale the hay for sale. Mr. Kerckhoff sent $500 to pay the local debts, and this made the future more cheering.

One of the rackets long worked by California promoters was selling dupes small tracts of land upon which the promoters agreed to plant trees and care for them for a share in the profits. They always secured worthless land and planted worthless trees, which they kept alive as long as the dupes continued to make payments. They could always persuade intelligent city people that the income from a few acres would supply ample means for a leisurely city life.

The Santa Fe Railway Company purchased a tract of land near the sea to experiment in growing eucalyptus trees for railway ties. This started a eucalyptus-planting boom fostered by numerous promotion schemes for growing every variety of eucalyptus for many purposes. None were ever profitable and were usually abandoned because it cost more to remove the trees than the land was worth.

A sanguine promoter interested the baggage agent of the new railway. They secured a tract of land near Otis, dug a well sixty feet down to water, and launched the Rio Virgen Eucalyptus Plantation Company. They hired three men and began a nursery to propagate young trees.

"They will only have to be irrigated three years," assured the promoter. "After that they will find their own water."

The baggage agent finally got wise. No more dupes were snared, and the promoter abandoned the project and left the men stranded. They sold Dix a team of mules, a wagon, and some implements for $50. Dix secured the outfit at daybreak and left before any creditors in Otis could intervene. He had possession and a bill of sale. They could only stew and cuss, which they did.

Altruistic souls now began pestering Dix with advice on matrimony. He could not understand why this should be deemed an obligation of a farmer. Dix had no income, but people assumed he did. George Mier was a local merchant and a school trustee. He and his wife were a happily married couple and scheming matchmakers. They were fine people. They were happy and earnestly desired to contribute to the happiness of others. A young lady teacher was secured for the Daggett school, and they assured Dix that they had carefully selected her for his special benefit and rhapsodized on the joy hymeneal bliss would give him.

This appalled Dix. He was bashful and girl shy. He never did learn the art of keeping a girl giggling and sniggering over fool sayings. He did not desire a wife. She might object to living in a rude shack in the desert and want him to move to town and get a job. Dix gave a display of cold feet.

However, Mrs. Mier had a fertile mind. Her small son had a wagon and pony. Occasionally he visited the ranch to secure milk. One day he appeared with the teacher, whom he introduced. After Dix placed the milk bucket in his wagon, the boy said giddap to the pony. Then, evidently remembering maternal instructions, he yelled "Whoa," stopped the horse, and turning to the teacher asked,

"Don't you want to stop here awhile and talk to him?"

The young lady was very much embarrassed. Hastily looking at her watch, she said it was getting quite late, and they must hurry back. The next day the Mier boy returned alone.

"Where is the teacher?" queried Dix.

"Mr. Van Dyke, are you going to marry that teacher?" he enquired.

"I don't know. I am thinking very seriously about it," replied Dix.

"Well, don't you do it. She ain't no good," he declared.

He declined to say more, but Dix now had a good alibi for not bestowing attentions.

The new railway was completed. Gangs of laborers no longer passed through, and local conditions returned to normal. The farmers raised a profitable hay crop that was readily sold in Daggett.

Like many newcomers to the desert possessed of visionary ideas, Dix was always in a hurry to acquire his first million dollars. Whenever he went to the village, he raced in at a fast gallop, riding bareback with a tie rope looped about the horse's nose. He usually tied up at the hitch rack in front of Mike's saloon.

Today as he yanked his horse up short, he noticed a small crowd on the sidewalk and an air of subdued excitement.

"What's up?" he inquired.

"Bert's killed a man," Doc Mc Farlane replied.

Dix looked about incredulous. Bert White, in the midst of the group, was plainly in distress, but he was only seventeen years old and had never quarreled with anyone. He was so good-natured that he never showed resentment, yet he had reported that he had deliberately shot a man through the head with a rifle. Old Bob, with a team and companion, had left for the scene thirty-five miles away to get the body. Bert was at liberty. It never occurred to anybody to file a complaint with the Judge or that Bert needed restraint.

The Pacific Coast Borax Company possessed many borax claims 130 miles north, in the Funeral Mountains bordering Death Valley. Under the terms of the government's mining laws, each year it was necessary to perform labor upon them to retain possession. On a small irrigated ranch at Furnace Creek, they raised alfalfa hay on the floor of the valley. Springs furnished the irrigation water, and Paiute Indians did the work. Few white men would stay during midsummer.

A twelve-mule freight team hauled supplies from Daggett. It was a ten-day trip, and few teamsters would drive even gentle mules without the aid of a swamper to assist in caring for them. There were no habitations along the route, and hauling water from wells with a rope and bucket and filling water barrels was arduous labor that had always to be done before retiring to sleep. This must be done for use in dry camps where there was no water.

Three days before the shooting, Shorty Smith's two-wagon freight team, with Bert as swamper, departed from the borax camp on the north side of the Calicos. The supplies could be transported to there by the branch railway that hauled ore to Daggett.

The first night's camp was a dry one on the Alvord Slope twelve miles beyond. There were eight miles of upgrade, with four of them strewn with sand that filled the tracks made by the last wagon that had passed, perhaps many days before. Such bad roads made necessary "doubling up," with only one wagon being hauled up a steep slope at a time.

The camping place depended upon when the teams became wearied. Any place was as good as another, just so it was far enough along to make possible the reaching of Garlock Well the next afternoon. This was twelve miles from the beginning of the slope. The last four being downgrade and easy. The "doubling up" actually made it a twenty-mile journey, and fifteen in a day was deemed fair.

13 THE MURDER STORY CONTINUES: BERT KILLS AN INSANE INDIAN ♦ CONTENTMENT ♦ At Garlock Well, there was a rope, a bucket, and an iron pulley wheel. The water was sixty feet down, a long haul. Here, the water barrels had to be filled, for the next camp was a dry one far up on the Granite Ridge, again just as far as the mules could travel before becoming wearied. The grade was steeper, but the road better. "Doubling up" was not necessary. Nor was there any choice of campsites.

Far up the Alvord Slope the freight wagons were overtaken by a livery team from Daggett bringing a passenger. Bert Lee was the son of a Paiute mother and an American father. For the past week in Daggett he had been engaged in the popular pastime of "blowing in a stake." He now wished to reach his home far out in the desert. Having learned of the freight team's departure, he had engaged the team and driver and thus overtaken it.

The livery team began its return journey, and the freight team proceeded on its way. The two freighters were glad to have Lee's company and assistance during the lonely journey that lay ahead of them. He was an amiable young fellow and well liked. He was well supplied with whiskey, but this did not lessen his welcome. Bert White was too young to care for it, but the teamster, Shorty Smith, enjoyed soaking in it.

Shorty was another of the odd characters then common on the desert. Naturally quiet and reticent, he never attracted attention when sober. A few drinks of whiskey always stirred his imagination, and he then began recounting wondrous tales of valor from his youth. He had been a famous Indian scout, serving under military commands, and had often engaged in bloody frays with Indians. His imagination never failed until either the whiskey or his hearers' patience ended.

After a few drinks of the whiskey generously dispensed by Lee, Shorty's yarning began, but it was not received with the derisive laughter of saloon loafers. Lee had lived all his life among Indians. His wits were addled by several days' drinking of adulterated bar whiskey, and he may have inherited some of the primitive passions of his mother's race.

Smith's tales infuriated him. Drawing his revolver, he ordered Smith to get off the wagon so he could kill him on the ground. Only the most abject pleas induced Lee to refrain from killing Smith. Lee consented to spare Smith's life if he would immediately depart on foot toward Daggett. Shorty Smith hurried out of gun range, and the team proceeded with Bert White driving and Lee menacing him. It was an appalling situation for even the bravest person inured to danger. Bert was not inured to anything. He was just a fun-loving boy marooned in a savage desert with an insane Indian.

Bert's mother was a poor widow who operated one of the dingy Daggett rooming houses. Bert was not old or strong enough to work in the mines, and he had been glad to get this job. Now he wondered whether he would ever again see his mother. He knew that Smith would reach the borax camp the next day and that an armed posse would quickly be sent after them. Lee knew it, too, and boasted of the murderous deeds he would do when overtaken. If he did not kill Bert in insane fury, the boy was liable to be slain in the battle that was impending. There was no escape for the terrified lad.

Late in the afternoon, the freight team arrived at Garlock Well. It was on the edge of a large, dry lake, in the bottom of a deep valley rimmed about by barren hills. It was not a cheery place at any time. Still menaced by Lee, Bert unhitched the team, tied the mules to the wagon, and began removing their harness. Lee had left his rifle on the high seat of the freight wagon where he could observe it and had retained his revolver. Going a short distance away, he squatted on his heels and, momentarily forgetting Bert, gazed meditatively at the ground. It was a desperate gamble with death, and only terror could have inspired Bert.

Quickly springing upon the wagon wheel, he grasped the rifle and fired. There was only one shell in it. A miss would have doomed him. He almost missed. The bullet struck Lee in the top of the head.

After feeding and watering the mules, Bert mounted one and returned to the borax camp. It was a lonely, dismal ride over the desert. On the way he overtook Smith. Shorty was not taking any chances. When he heard the mule approaching, he fled away from the road and hid. He thought it was Lee seeking him.

The Coroner came and held a perfunctory inquest. A jury exonerated Bert, and Lee was buried in the dismal graveyard on the mountain slope above Daggett.

Far out in the desert, from the base of a small hill of lava rocks, a large stream gushes out and waters a natural meadow and groves of mesquite trees. Long ago the emigrants on the Old Spanish Trail tarried there to rest, and the spot became known as Resting Springs. It had long been the home of Philander Lee, who had dwelt in the desert for forty years. Here with his Paiute wife he had long made his home and raised a family. A well-built house of stone and adobe housed them, and with the spring waters he irrigated small fields and raised much of the family's food. From his slender means he had hired a young American woman to dwell with them and educate his sons and daughters.

He had many friends, and a telegram to the railhead at Ivanpah sent a horseman coursing over the desert to Resting Springs. Two days after his arrival there with the tragic news, a grief-stricken old man drove a worn and jaded team into Daggett. When kindly friends told him of the circumstances that attended his son's death, he sent for Bert and with tears streaming down his face expressed forgiveness for his son's slaying. He assured Bert that neither he nor any of his family would ever bear him ill will and that they would always be friends. The pathos of it caused all present to weep.

The Judge was cheered by the alfalfa yields. He wrote to his friend Mills:

> The first cutting gave fifty-one loads from twenty-four acres. The average was greatly reduced by several acres of young stuff that last year lost half its growth by the loss of water. Also, by alkali spots not yet filled up by old enough plants. The oldest part ran over three tons to the acre. I can gamble on ten tons to the acre for the year but am satisfied I can do still better. I expect to cut 200 tons this year.

After some grumbling about doing his own cooking and being eaten by flies in a wooden tent (the shack), he ended with optimistic prophecies of future success.

The fourth summer ended, and winter approached. Eating canned grub continued to exasperate the Judge, but now they had plenty of milk and eggs, and his health had improved so much that his appetite was good and he could enjoy a hearty meal. He attended to the irrigating and other tasks. He kept active most of the day and slept soundly through each night. Occasionally, he rested on the veranda and read his tomes written in ancient Greek and Latin.

The debts had worried him. Arthur Bent, the contractor, had refrained from placing a lien upon the property because the Judge had promised his payment. This had worried him. It was another of those things he termed "an obligation of honor." Kerckhoff had given Bent promissory notes in payment. They were good collateral at any Los Angeles bank, and they satisfied Bent. In time, Kerckhoff paid them.

The Judge never harped on sin, but occasionally he gave his son a dissertation upon honor:

"Don't make promises unless you are sure you are going to be able to fulfill them.

"If a man cuts off your credit, don't you go elsewhere and pay cash. You spend your money where you got credit.

"Whenever you borrow money from a friend without security or interest, you repay it with the first money you get. Let others wait."

1. Daggett about 1906. When the Van Dykes settled there in 1901, Daggett was a wild and woolly frontier town, raucous with silver miners and land speculators. Standing in center of photo is Dix's friend, the famed frontier character Death Valley Scotty. He claimed to have a fabulously rich gold mine north of Daggett and for years kept its location secret. Only decades later was it discovered that Scotty's wealth came from an eccentric millionaire in Chicago.

The buildings face the railroad tracks, directly behind the camera to the south. The building immediately to the left of the Restaurant–Daggett Hotel is the Ryerse store, mentioned in the text and destroyed in the fire that swept the town in 1908. In the right of the photograph is a portion of one of Daggett's oldest buildings, the handsome Old Stone Hotel, standing today and scheduled for restoration.

Compare these buildings with those in the contemporary view in photo 20. Things have not changed very much in Daggett. (*Credit: Mojave River Valley Museum*)

2. Dix's father, Judge Theodore Strong Van Dyke, on the porch of his ranch house. In a mostly lawless land, the position of justice of the peace was at once prestigious and dangerous. Judge Van Dyke was willing to back up his legal opinions with firearms if necessary. When asked by a brother visiting from the East if he feared revenge from the toughs he sent to jail, Theodore replied, "Whenever a man gets to thinking of things like that, it is time to quit being Judge." *(Credit: Alan Golden)*

3. Rawboned determination on the desert. Left to right: daughter Mary, father Theodore, and son Dix. Mary later married a local prospector, George Golden. Strangely, Dix never mentions his sister in his memoir. *(Credit: Alan Golden)*

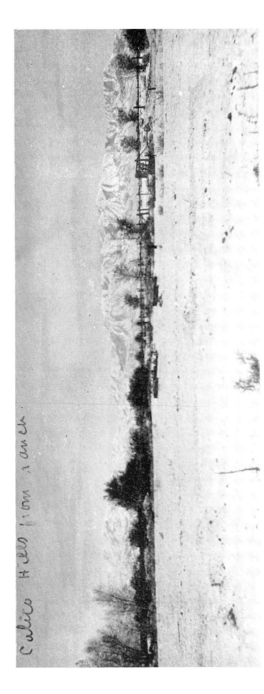

Calico Held from ranch.

4. Looking north from the Van Dyke Ranch to the Calico Mountains, six miles away. In the largest silver strike in Southern California's history, millions of dollars of ore poured out of the Calicos, turning Daggett into a wild town. *(Credit: Alan Golden)*

5. A present-day view of Green Oaks, birthplace of Theodore and the original family mansion on the outskirts of New Brunswick, New Jersey. *(Credit: Linda Bayless)*

6. In 1868, Theodore's father moved the family to Wabasha, Minnesota. The large house he built stood magisterially on a bluff overlooking the nearby Mississippi River.

7. Hay-cutting time at the Van Dyke Ranch in 1910. Left to right: John C. Van Dyke, Theodore, and Dix. *(Credit: Alan Golden)*

8. In contrast to Theodore's humble circumstances on the crude frontier, brother John C. Van Dyke, as seen here during a visit to the ranch about 1930, continued in the family's aristocratic tradition. A member of the East's *bon ton*, he was an influential art critic, author of *The Desert*, and art advisor to Andrew Carnegie, the richest man in America. Once when Uncle Jack visited the ranch, unschooled nephew Dix quipped: "He was a scholarly, dignified gentleman who taught book larnin' in a college and wrote books on art and nature and various highbrowed subjects." These tamarisk trees, a species imported from the Middle East, were planted at the ranch by Theodore and Dix for their beauty and shade. *(Credit: Alan Golden)*

9. John C. Van Dyke (right) in northern Mexico in 1900. Though he probably got much of the information for *The Desert* from his brother, outdoors authority Theodore, John C. Van Dyke also traveled extensively throughout the Southwest. This is the only known photograph of him while he was on the travels that led to publication of his famous desert book. *(Credit: Special Collections and University Archives, Rutgers University Libraries)*

10. Dix (left), Theodore, and early automobile on a ranch road. The coming of the automobile to the Mojave rang the death knell of frontier ways, though, as Dix reminds us, because of bad roads and lack of facilities, automobile travel across the desert remained perilous for years. *(Credit: Alan Golden)*

11. Isolated though it was, the Van Dyke Ranch served as a crossroads for lively intellects. On the right stands John Muir, well-known nature writer, explorer, and a founder of the Sierra Club. At center is Dix Van Dyke, and behind him, his father, Judge Theodore Strong Van Dyke. The two women at the left are likely John Muir's daughters, Helen and Wanda. *(Credit: New Brunswick Theological Seminary, Gardner A. Sage Library Archives. Used by permission.)*

12. A typical view of the Mojave Desert in the Daggett area. The dry bed of the Mojave River, center. Bare mountains and sandy sweeps make this one of the most barren landscapes in the United States. It also is a landscape of many subtleties and sometimes dramatic surprises. *(Credit: Peter Wild)*

13. A land of contrast: the Mojave has groves of enormous palms and thick stands of Joshua trees, such as those pictured here near Yucca Valley. Their wild appearance and bizarre branchings reminded early Mormon pioneers of the exhortative Old Testament prophet. *(Credit: Peter Wild)*

14. Casa Del Desierto, one of Fred Harvey's more lavish accommodations for tourists and a main feature of the expanded railroad facilities at Barstow mentioned by Dix. Built in the pseudo-Moorish style, this great building of turrets and arcades looms on the desert beside the railroad tracks at Barstow, six miles from Daggett. Here, in a highly unusual meteorological event, fog swirls around the Casa Del Desierto, now scheduled for restoration. *(Credit: Peter Wild)*

15. About a mile west of the Van Dyke Ranch, local historian Clifford Walker points to Indian petroglyphs etched into a lava rock on the flank of Elephant Mountain. *(Credit: Peter Wild)*

16. The Mojave Desert is dotted with playas, or dry lakes. These are low places filled with water only during times of snowmelt in the mountains or rare, heavy rains. This is Bicycle Lake, with the Tiefort Mountains in the background, now part of the army's vast Fort Irwin National Training Center. Teamster Dix mentions passing here when hauling supplies on the grueling trail north to the mines in Death Valley. *(Credit: Peter Wild)*

17. A freight train going east toward Needles enters Caves (Afton) Canyon, where Dix sometimes kept a herd of cattle. The bridge crosses the Mojave River, its dark flow seen to the right of the trestle. *(Credit: Laura Howard)*

18. Up in the mountains six miles north of Daggett is the former mining town of Calico. A hundred years ago, Calico's bonanza of silver flowed through Daggett, creating its prosperity. Restored by the wealthy Knott family in the 1950s, this authentic attraction now is run by San Bernardino County. From its hilltop perch, Calico's charming, one-room schoolhouse, complete with bell tower and desks waiting for students, overlooks the town and shows that more than greed was on the minds of Calico's residents. *(Credit: Peter Wild)*

19. A panorama of Calico and the desert beyond. The narrow-gauge train takes visitors on tours past the old stone houses and mine shafts dotting the surrounding hills. The main part of Calico is off to the right. The view beyond is breathtaking in its bleakness. Few people are likely to notice, or even less to visit, the little town of Daggett in the far distance. Hunched on the south bank along the green band of the Mojave River, Daggett is about an inch to the left of Elephant Mountain, the dark, lava mass appearing top right. *(Credit: Peter Wild)*

20. In the center of Daggett, at the Desert Market, on Santa Fe Street. One of the few businesses surviving in town, the Desert Market faces the railroad tracks, behind camera. Note the date, 1908, visible above the marquee. This was Frank and Homer Ryerse's general store, mentioned by Dix. It burned down in the fire of 1908 that swept much of the town and was rebuilt as a concrete structure. Compare with photo 1. The last building down the street is the Old Stone Hotel, reduced to one story by the same fire. *(Credit: Peter Wild)*

21. Dix chuckles that in his day Daggett had plenty of saloons but no churches. Now the town has one church, the Trinity Assembly of God, but no saloons. *(Credit: Peter Wild)*

22. A few hundred feet north of Daggett's one church is the broad bed of the Mojave River, center. The timbers sticking out of the sand in the foreground show the remains of an old borax-processing plant. Other facilities were directly across the river. A narrow-gauge railroad crossed the lower slope of Elephant Mountain, left of center, and brought the borax ore down from the area of the Calico Mountains, in the distance. What appear as two white squares to the far left, on Elephant Mountain, are water tanks, part of Daggett's present-day water system. *(Credit: Peter Wild)*

23. Graveyards can be important resources, windows into the character of the past. The grave of Alex Falconer, owner of the Bucket of Blood Saloon. *(Credit: Peter Wild)*

24. The Daggett Ditch as it passes, now unused, through the town of Daggett. The Daggett Ditch was the lifeblood of the Van Dyke Ranch. Four miles upstream from the ranch, water came to the surface of the Mojave River. From there, Dix channeled the water into the ditch, which followed the south bank of the river, ran through Daggett, then (less than a mile east of town) watered the orchards and alfalfa fields at the ranch. *(Credit: Peter Wild)*

25. At the Van Dyke Ranch, the last house where Dix lived. Though it is surrounded by the artifacts and curiosities Dix collected, such as the old wheel in the foreground, the house itself has been extensively modernized since Dix died in 1952. Despite this, or perhaps because of it, stories of ghosts continue to swirl about the house. *(Credit: Peter Wild)*

26. The old Daggett jail, preserved by Dix, stands near the front yard of photo 25. Left to right: Tracer, the ranch dog, with a ball in his mouth; Peter Wild; and Beryl Bell, local historian and keeper of the Daggett Museum. *(Credit: Laura Howard)*

27. The ranch grounds are dotted with various houses, many of them now in ruins, where ranch hands and guests stayed. This is the Bottle House. The circles in the walls are the butt ends of wine bottles thrust into the mud bricks. This is the place where Walter Fiss, radical political thinker and accomplished photographer, lived. To the right is one of Dix's old wagons and Tracer, the ranch dog. *(Credit: Peter Wild)*

28. Celebrated writer and naturalist John Burroughs visits young botanist Mary Beal in 1911 at her tent house on the Van Dyke Ranch. *(Credit: Harold and Lucile Weight Collection, the Mojave Desert Heritage and Cultural Association. Courtesy Dennis G. Casebier.)*

29. Ruins of the house where Mary Beal, pioneer desert botanist, once lived. She came to the Van Dyke Ranch in 1910 for her health and stayed until she died in the 1960s. Judge Dix Van Dyke officiated at the wedding of nephew Alan Golden at Mary Beal's house in the early 1950s. *(Credit: Peter Wild)*

30. Casa Desierto, the mansion built by Buel Funk and his wife, Helen Muir Funk, after John Muir died. Perhaps the most expensive private home within a hundred-mile radius, it stood within sight of the Van Dyke Ranch and in lavish contrast to the workmanlike buildings at the ranch. Pictured, left to right, are two historians from Barstow: Germaine L. Moon and Clifford Walker. *(Credit: Peter Wild)*

31. Lost to memory is the year that the original Van Dyke ranch house burned. The two patches of cactus, center, grow in the slight depression where the cellar was. The heavy wooden frame sunk into the ground near the camera is the remains of the scale used to weigh hay, sold by the ton. *(Credit: Peter Wild)*

32. Dix's nephew, Alan Golden, stands beside the ruins of the second Van Dyke ranch house. He was born here in 1932. A few months after his birth, mice gnawing kitchen matches set the wooden house afire. Tinder dry from the desert air, it went up so quickly that Mr. Golden's mother, Mary Van Dyke Golden, almost didn't have time to rescue her new baby. *(Credit: Peter Wild)*

These were some of his injunctions to his son.

Like most parents he had at times wondered whether his son would "be any count." The son never manifested a desire to stick to a steady job, and his father did nothing about it.

"I will not ask anyone to give you a job until you demonstrate you can hold one working for strangers," he declared.

Dix never tried to demonstrate. He did not like jobs. It irritated him to serve others for pay. But now he had been working hard for four years without any pay and only meager living. An occasional nickel cigar satisfied his yen for a sporting life. The little leisure he indulged himself with was mostly spent in reading various magazines, of which they received many. The local sports considered him stingy. He did not care what they thought. One of the compensations of his mode of life was that he did not have to care for anyone's opinion. It was not an easy life, but he was his own boss, with no one to order him about, and he need not be a supplicant for anyone's favor.

There was yet 500 feet of pipe to lay. A ditch for it had to be dug in the wet, sticky mud of the canal that had been deposited by the summer rain the year before. The soft mud walls of the new trench kept collapsing. The crew had to pile two parallel rows of brush on each side of the trench to hold back the ooze. Dix worked all winter at the job with one or two helpers. They lived in a tent and cooked their grub over a woodstove. They camped near an arrowweed thicket and soon were raided by mice from the brush. They trapped forty mice before the nuisance ended.

The job was hard and disagreeable. One began work at daylight on a cold winter morning, working in rubber boots and shoveling soft mud that stuck to the shovel. One soon acquired the knack of giving the shovel a flip that would slide the mud off, but none of the hobo helpers stayed long. When they had earned a "road stake," they quit. The job was at last finished, and the 500 feet of pipe laid and covered with gravel shoveled in from the sides of the canal. The bottom of the joints lay in shallow water and were not cemented. The pipe was lower than the water levels, and water flowed into the pipe.

Flood protection was another problem. The river's current struck directly against the canal heading, and levees extending out from the bank had to be built with teams and scrapers and then fenced with bundles of brush laid where the stream would strike. The bundles were anchored with wire to posts on the other side of the levee.

The new year of 1906 began auspiciously. A small flood came down the river and lasted a long time. It raised water levels and ensured plenty of water for another season. The alfalfa showed more promise, and the Judge was confident of heavier crops than the previous year. He was still determined to grow vegetables.

"The trouble with the garden is we irrigated it with furrows," he declared. "If we had flooded it, the manure would not have burned the crops. We will fix it right this time."

The land was regraded into strips, separated by borders, and the vegetables planted on the flat strips. They grew all right. So did Bermuda grass. Little grass had grown the previous year, not enough for it to be regarded as a pest. It was now. Conditions were now just right for its growth, and by midsummer the garden looked like a thick, thrifty grass lawn.

The seed came in with the imported hay, and for years it lay in the corrals without losing its germinating power. The Judge was mad. He made some unprintable remarks about things in general, but his grouch did not last long. There was too much hay to care for. It distracted his attention and consoled him. Also, his health was still good, and he could enjoy his food.

With the exception of Kerckhoff, none of his associates now possessed any money. In the beginning, Dieterle promised to contribute. He then had a high-salaried job that he later lost because of devoting some of his time to promoting a company to manufacture liquid air. Rhea had declared that he should sell out on long time-payments. Now Rhea was in the same predicament as Dieterle, without money, but he took a different view of his case.

He wanted to stay in. He had long been a victim of the incurable optimism the desert inspires in some people. The Judge was vexed:

"I did not come out here to operate a one-horse layout!" he growled.

He and Dix were supposed to draw wages from the net profits. So far there had been none. The two lived on the Judge's meager salary and the occasional sale of one of the Judge's manuscripts to a magazine.

The meager living conditions did not worry them. They were naturally lovers of the outdoors and regarded a house merely as a shelter to crawl into when the weather was unpleasant. The mere fact that they were able to live together and enjoy each other's company consoled them for trivial discomforts. During most of his life the Judge had satisfied his desire for recreation by hunting and fishing in almost virgin fields of sports. At other times he had experienced much pleasure in study and reading. Dix was not inclined to study boring subjects, but he was an omnivorous reader of almost everything he could get.

He pined for the lack of a library, but he had never liked a town and now enjoyed the rather primitive life they were living. They desired a farm that would be a home and a source of support, but neither cared very much for anything that money alone could supply. They did not care a hoot about money to spend on themselves. They did want it to develop more water and plant more alfalfa. They firmly believed that if they could get one hundred acres producing there would be sufficient income for future improvements and expansion of acreage.

14 FLAMBOYANT TALES OF TREASURE ♦ IMITATORS OF JUDAS ♦ A CONCEALED REVOLVER ♦ During the past five years a mining boom had been gathering volume in Nevada. It began with rich gold discoveries at Tonopah, on the desert about 300 miles north of Daggett. Gradually, the boom moved south with the marvelous gold discoveries at Goldfield and was now flourishing in the mountains adjacent to Death Valley. No laws restricted the operations of unscrupulous promoters, and innumerable corporations, many of dubious merit, were floated all over the United States to work the Nevada mines.

From every direction money poured in while wild tales of treasure flowed out. Such booms had occurred before, but this was the last. It was really the last of the frontier.* Just three years before, some hopeful promoters tried to interest capital in a proposed Daggett and Tonopah Railway. They had failed.

The Pacific Coast Borax Company had begun building a road for traction engines to haul borax from their Death Valley mines to Ivanpah. This was the end of a branch railway beginning at the main line of the Santa Fe Railway at a point one hundred miles east of Daggett. It was built before the Nevada boom to serve various camps in the desert.

Flourishing conditions now caused the abandonment of this project. Instead, investors created the Tonopah and Tidewater Railway Company, sold bonds to finance the cost, and began construction at Ludlow, forty-five miles east of Daggett. The new railway to Salt Lake City began building a branch line from Las Vegas to Tonopah. Those roads were completed, and years later after the boom collapsed, they were abandoned and the rails torn up.

Optimism was as thick as dust in a desert windstorm. From every direction came glowing reports of rich mines. High on top of the Funeral Range, where one could look down upon Death Valley, there was a shallow deposit of copper ore. A wealthy mining corporation sunk a hole 1,400 feet deep and proved there was little ore. For a time, Greenwater was a boom camp that had a newspaper. Water was costly and had to be hauled long distances, but the optimism lasted until the payrolls ended.

The Greenwater Kid was a young fellow who happened to locate a claim at the beginning. He sold it for $15,000 cash. It was a wonderful stake for a young fellow beginning his career. It spoiled the kid. Thereafter he loved to reveal his store of mining lore to loafers in saloons. He was a generous soul, and he often called upon the bar-

---

*Lee catches some of the madcap, surreal abandon of the last big boom, along with the irony of the bust: "Motorists riding across Death Valley by moonlight, top-hatted millionaires coming in by Pullman, ladies fancied up in furs and feathers at the fashionable Montezuma Club—these indeed represented a new kind of desert rat. Hardy old prospectors like Jim Butler, John McBride, Dan Kelsey and Shorty Harris looked upon them with mixed pity and disdain, and were not unhappy when the panic of 1907 came along and put an end to the show" (179).

tender to "fill 'em up again." He never lacked an audience acclaiming his wisdom. He thought he was a promoter until his money was fooled away and he had to go to work for wages. Long after that, he acquired a wife and five kids and died from a fall off a truck.

A rich gold strike was reported at Ord Mountain fifteen miles south of Daggett. The owners built a mill and spent much capital in futile efforts. Long after they quit, they claimed their superintendent had deceived them about the ore values, but now they were full of optimism.

"In a year's time," their manager prophesied, "there will be more mines operating around Ord Mountain than in any camp of its size in the United States."

The wisdom found many believing ears.

Sixty miles north, on the barren slopes of the Avawatz Mountains, surveyors laid out the townsite of Crackerjack. Flamboyant ads in the Los Angeles papers offered "choice lots for sale." The town consisted of a few tents, and water had to be hauled seven miles, but trifles like that were nothing. It was "destined to be the richest camp of all." And only a deep enough well was needed to ensure plenty of water. The first successful auto stage to operate on the desert was established. One touring car furnished transportation, and the fare between Daggett and Crackerjack was $25. The traveler either paid that or went by team, and it was a two-day journey. The traveler camped wherever night overtook him.

Daggett became infested with a coterie of mining promoters. Their mining activities were confined to the sidewalk between the saloons. There were more imaginary shafts and tunnels dug there than real ones in the surrounding terrain. Mining flourished best on days when some live ones were "setting them up." One of the enthusiasts was George Willis. He owned some wildcat claims at Ord Mountain which he had refused to sell for a large price.

"George," the Judge inquired of him, "is this all true about a rich strike at Ord?"

"Judge," in a confidential whisper he replied, "the half has not yet been told."

A miner's wages in the Nevada camps was four dollars a day, and Chinese were barred from the new camps. The same wages were paid at Crackerjack. There were only two mines hiring labor, and they employed only a few men. One of the mines hired a Chinese cook. The employees did not object. They were glad to eat his grub. It was better than that of the hobo cooks previously employed. They wanted the Chink to stay. Not so some incipient millionaires who possessed mining claims in the locality. They had to stew their beans, and batching tends to make men cranky. They could not afford to eat Chink cooking, and the sight of the Chink pained them.

They held an indignation meeting, and they decided that the dignity of the camp could only be maintained by enforcing the rules of the Nevada mining camps. The miners resolved that "The Chinese Must Go." Eight well-armed men descended upon the metropolis and announced their decision. They were not proletarians but landed proprietors performing a public duty. If there had been adobe houses, the Chink's employers might have decided the edict, but tents are poor defenses, and the Chink was loaded on the outgoing stage. Mr. Florman, a loud-talking gentleman who always wore a gun, defied the vigilantes and declared he would get himself a Chink cook. He did not have one, so they ignored his squawking.

The mining company tried to have the vigilantes prosecuted, but the county authorities brought about a compromise, and the Chink was allowed to return.

Two of the vigilantes claimed ownership of Drinkwater Spring, where water was secured. They ensconced themselves there and proclaimed that all comers must pay one dollar a barrel for water. A well-armed and indignant gang from Crackerjack descended upon them, and after indulging in dire threats, they filled their water barrels and left. The claimants did, too. The opposition was too strong for them. So much ill feeling was engendered that the rival town of Avawatz City was founded two miles distant from Crackerjack. A cold winter descended upon the desert. Five feet of snow fell at Crackerjack, which was over 4,000 feet high. The only fuel was branches of the creosote bush, a good fuel but difficult to gather in deep snow. The miners spent a miserable winter. Most of those who could not seek refuge in a mine tunnel went down to adjacent Death Valley or elsewhere.

The Frenchman who had endeavored to persuade the Judge to plant buckwheat had what he deemed a valuable cement claim near Crackerjack. Instead of doing assessment work, he had on the first day of each year filed a new location notice upon the claim. This was a common practice respected by local custom. It was very rarely that a contender tried to "jump the claim" by filing a prior notice. The Frenchman was ill, but fearful of losing his claim to some stranger, he made the arduous trip by team, and after his arrival in Crackerjack he died from exposure. Someone hired a team of mules and a light wagon from the ranch to go to Crackerjack. The dead Frenchman was loaded in, the brake blocks removed from in front of the wheels to prevent snow from clogging them, and the sixty-mile journey to Daggett made without an overnight stop. This procedure angered Dix.

"No one cares for that Frenchman. He has no relatives. Why couldn't you bury him out there instead of nearly killing my mules hurrying in here to bury him?"

This seemed to be a strange idea that never occurred to anyone.

That winter the Nevada mining boom began its collapse, but the effects were not felt in Daggett until the financial panic of 1907 descended upon the whole country. That finished the mining boom. The local promoters cheerfully proclaimed that another year would see local mining booming. They continued to dig imaginary holes in the Daggett sidewalk. The saloons were supposed to be selling soft drinks. Only two remained. The owners of the third had purchased a saloon in Barstow and removed there. Liquor was still surreptitiously sold. The price of beer had gone up.

Another election was held in November 1906. Again the granting of liquor licenses was an issue. The former saloonkeepers were very confident of winning. They carefully canvassed the list of voters and received assurances of support from the majority. They were to learn that some were imitators of Judas. To be sure, they had some former residents register and arranged for their return on election day. Dix learned of this the night before the election. He was young and brash. He did not wish saloons reestablished, nor did the merchants and best citizens. During the past two years, it had been a quiet and tranquil village. Those who sold liquor illegally kept drunken customers quiet and off the streets. The merchants sold more goods and collected many delinquent accounts. Most of the village soaks did not wish saloons. They had found it easier to leave booze alone without them.

Heedless of consequences, Dix volunteered to spend election day at the polls and challenge illegal votes. He did not expect help, for no one desired to incur the ill will of the wets.

Doctor Linhart was a middle-aged adventurer who had roamed about the world. Driven from Manchuria by the Russo-Japanese War, he had been attracted to Daggett by the prospective mining boom. He was lucky enough to locate and sell a claim for $2,500. It was bad luck for him. It caused him to spend several years locating more claims and making futile endeavors to sell another. He had taken the place of Doctor Mc Farlane, who had moved elsewhere. Doctor Linhart cared nothing about anyone's ill will and feared no one. Learning of Dix's intention, he volunteered to join him.

The Judge returned from a visit to Los Angeles in time to learn of his son's plans.

"Go ahead," he said. "Challenge all of them."

It was an unpleasant day for Dix. A surly, profane gang of wet voters congregated on the sidewalk in front of the polls and made nasty remarks about the challengers. Yet they stayed there all day, and Dix began to wonder if he'd have a fight on his way home. His courage was bolstered with a concealed revolver, but the suspense was annoying.

Linhart was serene and unperturbed.

"It don't bother me none," nonchalantly remarked Doc.

Only three voters were challenged. Others did not attempt to vote. There were two voters who had been away for two years. John Maupon and Howard Hinkle were cronies of Alex Falconer and always blew their stakes at his place. When they were broke, their credit was good, and they always paid their liquor debts. It was certain that Alex had paid their expenses to return and vote. Maupon solemnly swore that Daggett was his home, and the election board allowed him to cast his ballot. Hinkle balked. Several times he reappeared, resolved to take the oath, but each time he declined to be sworn. Finally in disgust, he tore his ballot to fragments and threw it into the street.

15 A NEW HOUSE ♦ THE FUNK CONFLICT BEGINS ♦ A GHOST MOANS ♦

When the polls closed, Dix went home. He had no desire to remain after dark. The atmosphere did not seem healthy, not with surly, intoxicated wets manifesting hostility.

The wets won by one vote. Someone picked up Hinkle's ballot and pieced it together. He intended to cast a dry ballot. If he had not been challenged, the vote would have been a tie, and the village, already dry, would have remained so for another two years. Hinkle was no prohibitionist. Long after, a small inheritance caused him to drink himself to death with moonshine whiskey, but he had a grouch about something and desired to retaliate.

Old Bob and the Judge had no opposition and were both reelected. A few disgruntled votes were written in for Billy Smithson, but his name was not printed on the ballots. Old Mike received a liquor license, but it was denied to the others, who had been convicted of illegally selling liquor. Al McRae, a wholesaler in San Bernardino, was granted a license, which enabled Alex to resume business as McRae's agent. Mr. McRae called upon the Judge, who in caustic invective portrayed a dismal future for him unless his saloon operated in a respectable manner. Mr. McRae placated him with promises of good behavior. The promises were kept, and the few who did get drunk were kept off the street.

During the previous winter, six inches of rain had fallen. It was double the normal precipitation and, coupled with a warm winter, produced a heavy crop of annuals all over the desert. The abundant feed caused a considerable increase in jack rabbits. Another wet winter was now bringing up the grass and causing a greater increase in rabbits for the year 1907. It also was a wet winter on the Coast, and the heavy precipitation on the mountains caused the river to flow steadily for several months. There was plenty of irrigating water, and prospects were rather rosy.

The farmers were now living in a new house built the previous year with a carload of lumber furnished by Kerckhoff, who among other ventures owned an interest in a lumberyard. There had been some acrimonious discussions over the house. The Judge desired to wait until they could afford to build a concrete house.

"What you want," he wailed, "is something just 10 percent better than we have now."

"We have been living in this miserable shack for five years. I'm sick of it," shot back Dix. "We can get the lumber now from Kerckhoff and build a decent house."

His insistence prevailed. The lumber was stacked for six months to allow it to dry thoroughly. A five-room house was built, with a double floor and a six-inch air space between the inner and outer walls. It was to be their home for a long time. Improvements were added to it. Eventually, it was destroyed by fire, together with quite a library and many keepsakes. Now its building caused a lot of idle gossip to the effect that Dix was building it for a bride.

Hugh Funk was an Indiana farmer who three years previously had emigrated to California, bought a farm near Los Angeles, and engaged in farming. He was a half brother of Dr. Rhea. Rhea, still reluctant to dispose of his interest in the Daggett ranch, prevailed upon Funk to sell his farm and join him in developing the desert enterprise. Mr. Funk had already paid a visit, and now he came again to discuss matters with the Judge.

Funk had $4,000 in cash and some workhorses. He desired to know whether Kerckhoff would advance any more money to match his.

"Mr. Van Dyke," he said, "I don't want to spend what I have and then get set here on the seat of my pants."

In time, he got to sell, all right, but now everything looked fine, and he left in high spirits. He returned later with his horses and began work.

Mrs. Funk came later. If she had any high spirits, her hubby got the benefit of them. He had concealed from her his intentions until he was too deeply committed to withdraw. She was accustomed to living in a puritanical rural community and looked askance at Daggett, which contained saloons but no church. She did not like the desert nor the shack the Van Dykes had abandoned.

She developed a grouch. Dix complained to his father that she was trying to brew trouble between him and a hired man.

"What you have to bear in mind," testily declaimed the Judge, "is that most women are darned fools. Don't pay any attention to her."

It was sage advice but not always easy to follow. The Funks were not readers of books or magazines, and there was never to be any affinity between the two families. Mr. Funk was a firm believer in hard work, and Dix relinquished the management of the ranch to him and confined his activities to things that would not bring him into conflict with his new associates. Mr. Funk cheerfully allowed him to do all the horseshoeing and blacksmithing.

The Crackerjack boom was still full of lusty life. An eloquent talker persuaded George Mier to sell him $1,000 worth of merchandise on credit to start a store at the camp. Another enterprising gentleman procured enough liquor stock somewhere to start a saloon. Mr. Mier secured for Dix the job of hauling the stocks to Crackerjack. He was to get $40 a ton for a three-ton load.

During the flood stage of the river, horses and wagons had used the railway bridge. There were few trains, and there had been no objections from the railway company. They would have been futile anyway. But now the river was low enough to ford, and a few wagons had done so and beaten a track. Dix started across with two wagons drawn by six horses. The river was always treacherous, and horses are ever inclined to turn and follow the swift current downstream. When in midstream, the leaders turned and could not be held by the lines. Funk's son, Buel, had been taken along as far as the river to assist in the crossing. Handing him a leather blacksnake whip, Dix yelled instructions to leap into the river and lash the leaders on their heads and straighten them out. Buel did it effectively, and the crossing was safely completed. If he had failed and the wagons had swung from the beaten track, they would have been mired in quicksand.

Buel was a mile from home, shivering in clothes wet with icy water coming from mountain snows. Dix broke open a case of bottled whiskey and poured some into Buel.

"I intended to show them that there was one teamster in this country who would not drink their rotgut," Dix grumbled, "but I don't want you to get sick walking home in wet clothes."

The second night's camp was at Coyote Wells, a rather dismal place where the northern slope of the Calicos met the edge of a great dry lake four miles wide. The shallow well contained salty, brackish water. It was deemed an eerie place. Some twenty years before, the superintendent of the Calico Mine was progressing on horseback from Daggett to Calico, carrying the mine's payroll. En route he encountered an ambitious footman who amazed the rider by flourishing a large revolver and depriving him of both horse and payroll. Such actions were unprecedented, and it had not occurred to the superintendent to avoid the robber. Pedestrians often walked the six miles between the two towns.

The next day the superintendent, accompanied by Johnny Ackerman and an Indian trailer, encountered the robber at Coyote Holes. Ackerman shot and killed him. Superstitious ones averred that the robber's ghost had been seen promenading about in the starlight. They would not camp there if alone.

Dix did not believe in ghosts, but he was lonely, and the company of his revolver tucked beneath his pillow was cheering. He retired late after filling his water barrels and caring for the team. He was restless and lay awake. Suddenly, a weird moaning sound caused him to bounce to his knees and clutch his pistol. He was not scared, but he was startled and prepared for wailing banshees or anything else.

It was only the siren horn on the approaching auto stage, but it was the first time he had heard one. The driver was alone and glad to chat and drink some whiskey.

The next night's camp was far up on the Alvord Slope. The desert wagons had wide tires so that they could roll on top of the sand and wheels sixty-two inches apart. On the other hand, autos had narrow tires and wheels fifty-six inches apart. Either one ruined a sandy road for the other. The auto preceded the freight team, and it had to break track up the sandy slope. This was exhausting work for the team, even though hauling one wagon at a time.

The team arrived at Garlock Well in the late afternoon. Dix was tired and thirsty. He had not known enough to carry a keg of drinking water from home, and for two days he had been drinking the salty water of Coyote Wells. Even this had been exhausted before his arrival. It was here sixty feet to water. The water tasted sweet. As each bucket was raised for the thirsty team, Dix took deep draughts. After several buckets, up came a drowned owl, followed by a dead jack rabbit. Each had been down there a long time. This was what he would drink for the next two days.

This was another dismal place, where not long before young Lee had been killed. Dix was cheered by the company of three prospectors who camped overnight nearby. He treated them to whiskey and cigars, and they assisted in filling the water barrels.

16

SOME GRUESOME TRAGEDIES ♦ "A FURIOUS BATTLE ENSUED . . ." ♦ THE FUGITIVE CAPTURED ♦ The road led up through rock-strewn Black Canyon, over four miles of the flat dry bed of Bicycle Lake and onward up the long slope of the Granite Ridge.* This was hard ground, and there was no more doubling up to do. On the lake, Dix left the trailing wagon, piled most of its load on the other, and proceeded. He had plenty of bottled beer and a canteen filled with strong, boiled tea. Neither was satisfactory. Both weather and beer were warm, and the tea produced reminiscences.

The long slope of the Granite Ridge had a south exposure and was now deeply covered with grass and flowers. In midafternoon, Dix

---

*As to the rather strange name of Bicycle Lake, around 1890, teamsters hauling a string of wagons loaded with borax across the usually dry bed of the lake were astounded to see a bicycle inexplicably sticking out of the dried mud (Keeling, 22).

grazed the team for two hours, and the journey continued until late at night. Crackerjack City consisted of a few tents, but the inhabitants gave a glad welcome, and the saloonkeeper, who had been impatiently waiting for his stock, dispensed hospitality. The only excitement was caused by a lizard running up a miner's pantleg. The victim emulated a quick-change artist and yanked his pants off in a jiffy. He denied being frightened and said he was just curious. The next day Dix had to make the fourteen-mile trip to Drinkwater Spring and back to secure enough water for the team.

Close beside the road leading up the slope of Avawatz Mountain was a cairn of stones forming a monument for another gruesome tragedy. A few years before, Jack Anderson and Issac Bateman had started on a prospecting trip. Near here, Anderson, who had been on an extended drunk, became seized with delirium tremens. Leaping off the wagon, he fled over the desert to escape his imaginary pursuers. Bateman went on a few miles to Cave Springs, where he secured help and returned. They failed to find Anderson, and one of the party, Philander Lee, went to his home at Resting Springs, thirty miles farther out on the desert, and returned with Indian trackers. They found Anderson's body and said his tracks showed that he had been watching the first party seeking him and had eluded them. The body was unceremoniously placed in a shallow grave and stones heaped on top. It was no place for a Coroner's inquest, nor could the Coroner have been induced to make the journey.

During the previous year, each of the farmers filed a Desert Land Claim on 320 acres of land adjoining the ranch. Under the law, it was necessary to perform $320 worth of work on each tract each year. Additionally, on the fourth year there must be forty acres planted to irrigated crops and a final payment of $1.25 made for each acre. Work was now begun grading land upon the Judge's tract. For the first time, Dix received pay for his labor. He and Funk each drew $75 a month from the funds that Funk invested.

Dr. Rhea was killed by a streetcar while riding a bicycle in the city of Long Beach. He was quite deaf and, not hearing the car, had ridden in front of it. His widow inherited his property and sold his interest in the ranch to Funk. Rhea was a fine, honorable man and well liked and respected by all who knew him. He had grieved very much over his folly in persuading many friends to invest in his unprofitable mining venture and had been anxious in some way to make enough to repay their losses.

There was a good hay crop, large enough to induce the buying of a newfangled baler. Like the old one, it was worked by horses. Power balers had not yet come into general use.

Rabbits were more plentiful, but the fence kept them out. During the previous year, Dix had occasionally ridden about shooting them from horseback with a .22 rifle. His horse soon learned to stop and stand still whenever Dix raised his rifle. This summer he again indulged in rifle practice. It was a good year for the farmers, but a calamitous one for Daggett and the incipient mining millionaires.

The completion of the Tonopah and Tidewater Railway caused the Pacific Coast Borax Company to abandon its Calico mines and transfer their operations to another borax mine in the Funeral Mountains bordering Death Valley. The American Borax Company at Daggett acquired a rich borax mine at Lanf, in the Soledad Canyon near the Coast, and they moved there. Both companies dismantled their mills and buildings. The Wheeler Borax Company, a small outfit mining borax in Odessa Canyon in the Calicos, just folded up and quit. Borax dropped in value from seven cents a pound to three cents, and only rich mines could operate. The borax companies had employed 200 men, and much of their earnings had been spent in Daggett. During this year, a British company invested a large amount in a mine and mill on the east end of the Calicos. They started before the slump, finished their construction work, and never operated. In time, their plant was torn down and sold for junk, and they quit business.

The financial panic of 1907 finished the mining boom. Unable to secure sufficient currency, most of the banks printed and issued clearinghouse scrip. Many of them afterwards surreptitiously bought it back at a discount through private agents. The scrip was unlawful, but the federal government tolerated it until the emergency was over and people began depositing their hoarded money in the banks.

Old Mike sold his saloon and other property and bought a home in a small town near Los Angeles. Mike did not wish to go. It had been his boast that he had not crossed the mountains between the desert and the sea in thirty years.

"As long as a man's contented, what in Hell does he want to go for?" he asserted.

However, his wife's wishes prevailed.

An old crony who visited him returned and said his condition was pitiful. His neighbors were all strangers to him, none cared for his society, and he could not have been lonelier on a desert island. He had always been a friendly soul who dispensed cheer among his desert friends. The ones he liked best were those who drank the least.

Old Bob was subject to irritable spells. One night a glib talker succeeded in borrowing a dollar from him. Later, learning that the borrower was ensconced in a brothel, Bob invaded the dive and compelled restitution of the dollar. He was no Puritan but was indignant because he had been deceived by false representations. He still nursed a grouch because he could not get a railway pass. In a fit of pique he released from the jail a prisoner Billy Smithson had arrested and locked in. Billy apprehended the escaped prisoner and jailed him elsewhere. Bob had committed a felonious offense and one which his office did not give immunity for. He had no more right than a private citizen to release anyone from jail. The mess ended with Bob resigning and Billy being appointed Constable.

The local borax mill had imported Louisiana negroes to work in the mill and borax vats. It was hard, disagreeable work that a white man disliked to do for the meager wages paid. A Louisiana white gentleman bossed the vat gang, and he had secured the negroes.

"It's a shame to make a niggertown out of this," remarked an indignant Irishman.

"I don't care as long as they stay niggers, and they always will as long as I boss them," retorted the boss.

Ginger Smith grew eloquent in revealing how "we handle niggers down in Missouri." His eloquence incensed the colored people enough to cause them to patronize the rival store.

"You are going to have trouble with those niggers," he admonished Billy Smithson.

Billy smiled tolerantly. He had been raised in the country and knew little of them. Most of them were well behaved, and Ginger was somewhat of a crank.

Another summer had waned, and Mr. Funk and Dix were hitching a horse to the driving cart to make an evening call in the village.

"What's that racket in town?" queried Dix.

"It sounds like the kids shooting off a bunch of firecrackers," replied Funk.

"That's not allowed. Dr. Rhea put in a stock one year, and the other merchants bought it all and set it off outside of town. They were mad at Doc," rejoined Dix.

When the two arrived in town, they saw an agitated crowd milling about in front of Mike's saloon.

"What's the matter?" inquired Dix.

"A nigger shot Billy," someone replied.

In the dancehall beside the saloon Billy lay upon a bench with four bullet wounds in him and his life ebbing fast. His young wife was sitting on another bench, struggling for self-control. Her agonized features indicated that she was almost breaking.

Nothing could be done except guarding nearby railway stations, but all through the night preparations were made for a manhunt to begin with daylight. Dix awakened Johnny Ackerman and requested his rifle.

"Is it all right?" he asked as he reached for it.

"Yes," replied Johnny. "I killed one man with it. You should be able to kill another."

That was the only allusion Johnny ever made to the slaying of the robber at Coyote Holes.

Ed Silver was an ex-soldier who for several months had worked on the night shift. That evening when he came to the mill, he had found a white man at his job and was informed by his boss, Mr. Millet, that he was discharged. He tried to strike Millet with a shovel and was knocked down with a wrench.

"I will get my gun and kill you," Silver threatened as he departed.

He was regarded as a "mean nigger" and was reported to be a good marksman with a revolver.

Mr. Millet hastened home for his gun and went to Billy's home for help. With another armed employee, they set forth seeking Silver. He had already called at Millet's home and enquired for him and was prowling about looking for him. They all met in a street back of Mike's saloon. It was a bright, moonlit night, with the shadow on Silver's right side. Concealed in his right hand was a small automatic pistol, beneath his coat a revolver. The trio approached him with Billy in front and Millet behind.

"Step out, Millet, I want to talk to you," called Silver.

"I don't want to talk to you," replied Millet.

"What is the trouble about Ed?" inquired Billy as he stepped forward.

A burst of gunfire was the reply. Millet had one gun, the other employee two. A furious battle ensued. Though wounded in the thigh, Silver escaped by running. Billy's gun was never found. Some loafers in the saloon were the first on the scene. One of them was supposed to have picked it up.

Ginger Smith and two others quickly ran a mile to a negro dwelling across the river. Silver had been there and left.

"Ginger, I did not suppose you had nerve enough to do a thing like that," a wag jeered.

"I was brought up not to be afraid of niggers," proudly retorted Ginger.

The next morning Silver was tracked up the river and into dense thickets of brush. A crowd vainly hunted the brush without discovering his concealment. That night he managed to board a freight train and got off in the Cajon Pass, the deep defile cleaving the mountains that separate the desert from the Coast. The third night he was walking through the pass. Four officers from San Bernardino, all friends of Billy's, were maintaining a vigil in the narrowest place. Silver walked into the trap and surrendered before he was recognized. Billy had been raised in San Bernardino, and fear of lynching induced the Sheriff to send Silver to Los Angeles for safekeeping.

The news of Silver's capture brought relief to the weary crowd at Daggett after a futile hunt of three days and nights. Billy had died a few hours after he was shot. There was nothing more to do except collect some money for his widow. Three hundred dollars was quickly collected. Everybody who could contributed.

17 A STORY TOO GOOD TO SPOIL ♦ JOHN MUIR CURSES ♦ SUCKERS AND DUPES ♦ Silver was sentenced to hang. The governor had been elected by the Republican vote of Los Angeles. There was a large colored vote there, for which both Republicans and Democrats contended. The colored politicians went to the Republican politicians, and they went to the governor. He commuted the sentence to life imprisonment. A few years later Silver died in prison.

The negroes were ordered to leave Daggett by a few bravos who stayed close to home. They were glad to go. One who feared Silver had spent three days and nights in the railway depot, snuggling close to a large revolver.

Word of Billy's demise spread along the railways, and the hoboes began congregating in Daggett and became a nuisance. The railway company sent another special officer to replace Billy. He was Fred Johnson, an obstreperous gentleman from Missouri, who quickly collaborated with Ginger on the race question. He gratified his obstreperousness by running the hoboes out.

Some wag spread the yarn that he had mistaken Old Bob for a bum and had ordered him to leave. Mr. Johnson denied this.

"That is too good a story to spoil," said the Judge to Johnson. "If I were you I would not deny it."

Johnson was appointed Constable despite the fact that he had not been in the state long enough to be legally eligible. But that was a trivial technicality that no one commented on.

Mining was now dead. There were few jobs. The new railways intercepted much of the desert trade. The promoters went with the crowd. Live ones rarely came to "blow a stake." The town dwindled to one store, one restaurant, and one saloon. Half the houses were abandoned.

The only monied man was J. B. Osborne, a strange character who alternated between wealth and poverty and died broke. Long ago he acquired mines at Tecopa, far out in the desert. Through hungry years when he lived on credit, he clung to the Tecopa mines. Now the building of the T & T Railway close by enabled him to sell them for a fabulous sum: $350,000 paid in cash. He had also clung to mines at Ord Mountain. Now he announced that he would work them. Long ago, he had invented steam traction engines that for many years had lain discarded. They were resurrected, reconditioned, and driven about the Daggett streets. Mining was begun and carried on in a desultory manner. Nothing came of it, but for a time it gave employment. Osborne should have retired. He was too old to cope with scheming sharpers. He had paid all of his debts, and when his money was gone he lived on credit until his end.

The year 1908 began auspiciously for the farmers. They had verbally contracted with a well-driller to drill two wells in the canal above the pipeline. They bought some casting, and the driller's creditors seized his equipment. No wells were drilled, but they had sufficient water. The river again flowed until late in the spring. There was still a market for all of the hay they could raise.

John Muir, the famous naturalist, brought his daughter Helen to the ranch to remain for her health. They were wealthy, and Muir decided to build her a dwelling house. He was Scotch and had in his youth endured extreme poverty. Though naturally a generous soul, he now displayed extreme penuriousness. It resulted in a tiny shack with one room and a porch. He made a bunk two feet wide for the nurse and was much provoked when that lady insisted on it being wider.

"These damn Dutch are all used to big beds full of feather ticks," he lamented.

Miss Muir imported a saddlehorse and shocked the village grannies, both male and female, by riding astride with a divided skirt.* It resulted in some acrimonious debates in which Dix joined. He hated sidesaddles because they caused sores on the backs of horses.

Again green grass and blooming flowers carpeted the desert. Two old-timers met in the village street:

"Andy," piped Mr. Robert Greer, "we've had three wet winters in succession now. That's something none of us old-timers ever saw before. I believe it's the Salton Sea doing it."†

"Well, Bob," rejoined Mr. Andrew Mc Shane, "it ain't that. It's these gol-durned railroads. They're running so damn many trains nowadays they're disturbing the air currents."

In June the rabbits became very numerous. They dug under the fence and finally learned to make holes in the wire. Shooting them produced results, until the rabbits learned to invade the alfalfa field after dark and leave before morning. Efforts to plug the holes were futile. Mr. Funk conceived the idea of having Buel patrol the fence all night with a lantern and close the holes. The next morning the field was full of rabbits running about and seeking a hole. None seemed to know how to make a hole to escape. Buel reported that during the night he had seen droves of them. He continued his patrol for two weeks.

Each morning at daylight all hands, on foot, horseback, and with dogs, herded the rabbits into pens and clubbed them to death. It may

---

*Helen's riding horse was sent by her father from the rural Muir home in northern California. To keep Helen company at the ranch, her father also sent a dog, named after the famous one celebrated in Muir's book *Stickeen*. For more on Muir and Daggett, see Wolfe (309-10, 327, 347-48).

†Inadvertently manmade, the Salton Sea is an example of nature kicking back in the midst of the mania for desert development. During 1905-6, engineers were constructing an irrigation project to draw water from the Colorado River south of Yuma, Arizona. The men stood aghast when the Southwest's mighty river suddenly leapt out of its bed and shot across the desert, devastating the Southern Pacific Railroad and destroying the homesteads of many new settlers, to fill a vast low place in Southern California. The Salton Sea lies 100 miles southeast of Daggett and about the time of Dix's mention covered 400 square miles.

have been sport for some, but not when it was followed by ten hours of arduous labor in the hay field. When the rabbits were being beaten to death with clubs, many cried in piercing shrieks like a tortured child. It was a rather sickening job, and it so disgusted Dix that several years elapsed before he could again eat a jack rabbit.

John Muir had made many long and solitary journeys among the Sierra Nevada Mountains equipped with a bag of bread and some tea. He would never catch a fish or kill any bird or animal. He would eat them when someone else prepared and cooked them. He had been a hunter in his youth but had developed an aversion to taking life. One morning he was enticed out to see the rabbits corralled. He was very much interested until they were penned and the slaughter began. Then in great disgust he retreated to the house.

"That was a very brutal exhibition," he declared.

The best day's kill was 465 rabbits. In two weeks, 4,000 were killed, and that seemed to be nearly all of those about the ranch. They continued to be numerous in other sections along the river and caused great destruction. In midsummer they became infected with what seemed a dysentery and died in great numbers. All of the cotton-tail rabbits disappeared for some reason that could not be discovered. Maybe they died, too.

The Judge's brother came from New Jersey for a visit. He was a scholarly, dignified gentleman who taught book larnin' in a college and wrote books on art and nature and various highbrowed subjects. He looked soft and grumbled about ill health but thought nothing of roaming about the desert on the hottest summer day for eight hours without a drink or anything to eat. He tried to demonstrate that he could keep out rabbits by closing their holes. The rabbits were not deterred, but he derived some gratification from clubbing some.

For a period of years both the federal government and private corporations had been constructing irrigation projects in the arid sections of the western states. A great canal was diverting water from the Colorado River into the Imperial Valley. Flamboyant articles filled newspapers and magazines describing the "marvelous fertility" of desert soils. Coupled with this was a lot of drivel about newly discovered methods of "scientific farming" and silly yarns about smart city men who engaged in farming with their rear pockets stuffed with literature on farming. They were demonstrating to rural yokels how the art should be performed. Anyone who had spent his life in a city clerking in a store or operating a shoeshine stand was deemed capable of understanding "scientific farming," but, of course, it was too abstruse for simple rural folk to grasp. Improvements in the gasoline engine made pumping water feasible, and rich oil discoveries in Southern California provided cheap fuel. It was a fine setup for unscrupulous real estate salesmen.

The procedure was to inform a sucker that the salesman knew where he could secure 320 acres of fertile desert land with various tributary advantages by merely making improvements and paying the government $1.25 an acre. All the agent desired was $1.00 an acre for showing the land and making out the filing papers. The sucker had to place his money in escrow for ninety days so that he could not swindle the agent by declining the land and then surreptitiously filing on it. It was a fine graft while it lasted, and gifted talkers and liars did well.

In 1906 newcomers were settling the desert lands adjacent to the upper end of the Mojave River. Many tracts were filed on by wealthy city people, some of whom invested large sums in improvements that gave no return. Many tracts were on high lands where the depth to water was between 200 and 500 feet.

There was plenty of land along the river, close to the railway and with water at shallow depths, but no one desired that. Mere trifles like the law of gravity did not interest them. In 1908 the land locators began operations near Daggett. The ranch there yielded marvelous crops of alfalfa irrigated by water coaxed through a long dirt ditch. After showing the dupes the alfalfa fields, it was easy to convince them that they could pump water from wells much cheaper. All the suckers desired to know was how many tons of hay were raised to the acre and the price it sold for. There was no use trying to tell them anything about the tribulations they would endure. That merely gained for one their ill will and the reputation for being "a knocker." New-comers usually believe that the old-timer desires to hog the country and keep them out.

Some of the locators desired Dix's assistance in fleecing and offered inducements. He curtly declined. He knew the dupes would lose whatever money they invested and wanted none of it.

"If I am going to rob people, I would rather stick 'em up with a gun," he growled.

Just the same it was irritating to see others gathering the easy money.

Otis had developed into a large village, and the name was changed to Yermo. On the west was a large area of level land. It was promptly filed on. To do the first year's assessment work, the new owners dragged it with railway rails to uproot the brush. This caused the windstorms to almost smother the village with dust. It made the women hard to live with and caused much profanity. Housecleaning followed every high wind. Wells were drilled, pumps installed, and houses erected, but no crops were ever raised.

It was an era of good times and speculation. Los Angeles had for several years been rapidly increasing in population, and many people became wealthy on increasing land values. Many of the land locators were mere speculators desiring to get cheap land they could sell at a good profit. Most of them seemed imbued with the belief that the government was making them a present of the land. This is a common fallacy. Few ever seem able to realize that the money invested to secure title to government land is part of the purchase price.

18 NOMAD WOMEN ♦ THE OLD WAYS DYING OFF ♦ THE VIRTUES OF A SCHOOLMARM ♦ THE PRICE OF BEER ♦ Despite the rabbit raids, a good hay crop kept all hands busy during the summer and fall. During the previous fall, oats had been planted in the alfalfa fields and a mixed crop of hay secured. This was sold to the new borax company building a mill near Yermo. To Dix fell the task of delivering it. He loaded six tons of hay on two wagons, coupled them together, and then awaited a windy day. When all labor ceased because of too much wind, he hitched on six horses and left home at four o'clock in the morning. The last mile was uphill. One wagon at a time was drawn up by the six animals. Then he had to unload the hay, care for the stock, and eat lunch. He reached home about 10 P.M. He did not like it, but no one else could drive so many horses.

The Van Dykes planted a small orchard of various kinds of fruits, and they stuck rows of cottonwood cuttings into the ditch banks. Another house was crudely built with reclaimed lumber from the wrecked borax mill. It housed Bill Swartz, who had come from Indiana to work on the ranch. He brought a wife and two kids. He was a good hand. Mr. Funk did not like native sons. Before accepting employment, the locals irritated him by enquiring how many hours they were expected to labor and what the wages would be.

"That makes me hot," he complained.

Five hundred feet of the pipeline awaited completion. After laying the pipe, the men filled the open canal several feet deep with debris. Late in the fall, they built a one-room shack near the work for cooking and sleeping. It served all hands except Dix, who preferred the open air. He was odd, anyway, and in the evenings read a book instead of playing cards with the others. The workers dragged most of the dirt up a twenty-foot bank with teams and Fresno scrapers. Railway ties were pointed on one end with an axe. Two rows were driven four feet apart, braces put in between, and a roof of railway ties laid on top. The whole was covered with a layer of gravel. Water filtered in through the cracks and increased the irrigation stream. The ties were driven down with a homemade piledriver operated with a gasoline engine. It was rather crude but effective work. After finishing the pipeline, Dix devoted the remainder of the winter to grading more land for alfalfa and other work. Again the river flowed during winter and spring, assuring plenty of irrigation water for the year 1909.

Conditions had changed at Camp Cady. Old Swanze died at the soldiers' home. Old Mudgett passed quickly under an attack of pneumonia, and Old Frank Parish, feeling that his end was not far off, quit and moved to town. He had long been on the charity list of George Mier, who had sustained him for many years. He had accumulated sixty head of cattle from a small herd heirs had purchased for him several years before. The cattle were given into the care of Ed Courtwright, the local liveryman. He was to receive half of the profits for caring for them. It gave Ed's kid brothers an excuse to ride the livery horses thin, until Ed's partner, Byron Rowan, stopped it. Byron was a mulatto and well liked. He had always lived among white people and knew how to get along with them. He was very suave and affable.

The son of a pioneer, Mudgett was one of the few survivors of the old tribe of hunters and trappers who preferred a meager existence free from the trammels of towns. He had a sure test for water. Once when encamped at Soda Lake, two cattlemen called after he had retired. Being a hospitable gentleman, Mr. Mudgett arose and insisted upon preparing supper for the weary travelers. After building a fire and placing a skillet on it, he solicitously enquired of his guests what kind of meat they preferred.

"Gentlemen," he quoth, "you kin have yo choice. There is cat, coyote, and badger."

With difficulty, his embarrassed guests persuaded him they had already supped.

Will Mudgett had worked a long time for the borax company and had saved his wages. He had persuaded Frank Ryerse, the local butcher, to invest in cattle and allow him to care for them on shares. After his father's death, he was unwilling to remain at Cady. The cattle were rounded up and delivered to Ryerse at Daggett. There were 140 head, and they had been gathered to count and also sell. Ryerse was persuaded to turn them loose and hire a man to care for them. The cattle returned to Cady but never received much care from anyone Ryerse hired.

Will's mother and sister arrived with a large herd of goats. Long before, the old folks had separated, and the girl went with the mother. The two roamed the desert with their goat herd until it became a large flock. They tarried for a while, but the feed was not good enough for the goats, and with Will they departed. Before leaving, they sheared the goats near the ranch.

At supper Miss Muir inquired, "What kind of a man is that goat herder?"

The Judge had tried to buy a kid to eat. Now he was chewing some tough meat and thinking how good a young goat would taste. Looking upward he said to her, "You might get a nice young kid out of that fellow."

The desert was changing from an old era to a new era. No one yet realized it. The change came about gradually. The old inhabitants of the desert were dying off and a new element replacing them. The old pioneers' ways, faults, and virtues were to become traditions.

In Daggett a smug-faced mutual admiration group developed. They displayed their piety by gathering in the schoolhouse on Sunday and indulging in noisy manifestations of righteousness. The poor schoolteacher had to join and teach a Sunday school class. There was no other diversion for them. Good-looking gals were rarely hired.

"We want a sensible woman to teach," declared the old grannies.

The older and homelier she was, the more sense she was deemed to possess. Occasionally, Dix would relieve his feelings by making caustic remarks to a school trustee, but they sassed back and told him it was none of his business how the school was managed.

Automobiles were no longer a curiosity. Frank M. Ryerse was using one to deliver meat to Yermo. Doctor Linhart invested in one that looked like a buggy. It had high, wooden wheels with narrow, solid rubber tires. It was nice-appearing but failed to travel over the desert roads. Joe Goodrich had been the master mechanic of the Pacific Coast Borax Company. He made a contraption to prospect with. On a wagon he mounted an air-cooled engine. Hitched it to a gear wheel fastened to the rear wagon wheels and traveled at the rate of ten miles an hour. His machine could traverse rough ground impossible for autos, and he used it for several years. Autos were yet temperamental creatures, and only good mechanics dared venture far from town in them. A transcontinental journey was still an endurance run made a few times a year and loudly ballyhooed by those who succeeded in reaching the Pacific Coast. In time autos were to revolutionize life on the desert.

Frank Ryerse bought George Mier's store and brought a cousin from Canada for a partner. The store burned one evening and caused more excitement than had happened since Billy Smithson's murder. Everyone in the village attended and rescued most of the stock. A new building of concrete costing $4,000 replaced it. This was the only new building erected during a period of twenty years.[*]

Jack Garrity was an Irish laborer who had worked on a railway construction gang in the Caves Canyon.[†] He located a mining claim there containing fluorspar. He fondly believed it to contain great wealth and continually descanted upon it. One day he appeared in the Ryerse store with a half-filled bottle of whiskey. The other half was under his skin. He set the bottle on the counter and began an oration about his mine. Some nasty-minded small boys sneaked the bottle into the back yard and diluted it, then brought it back. Jack finally felt the need of more stimulation and took a deep drink from the bottle. With a sour grimace he raised the bottle and smashed it on the concrete floor. Homer Ryerse charged forth from his office mad enough to fight and profanely demanded an explanation.

"That's all right, that's all right," replied Mr. Garrity as he backed out the door.

Homer saw the kids racing for the rear door, and he realized there was some mystery he did not understand.

Alex sold beer for two bits a bottle, a glass of beer for fifteen cents, or two glasses for two bits. He was too penurious to use a whole bottle for two drinks. If he opened a fresh bottle to sell two drinks, he left

---

[*]One of the few businesses in Daggett, the store, on Santa Fe Street and now called the Desert Market, remains open. A niche above its marquee clearly shows the date 1908, the year of the fire and the subsequent reconstruction of the store.

[†]Now known as Afton Canyon. Located about thirty miles east of Barstow off Interstate 15, this "Grand Canyon of the Mojave," a labyrinthine tangle of canyons, is well worth a visit. Take the Afton Road turnoff.

half a drink in the bottle. The next customer got it with another half drink of fresh beer added. The next customer got the stale beer remaining in the bottle. A stranger, indignant at this procedure, made vituperative remarks to Alex about this. But Alex was immune to insults, kidded the protestant along, and gave him another drink gratuitously. Then a loafer, getting the wink from Alex, set up the drinks. Before long, the stranger was buying drinks regardless of cost.

The ranch bought the Ryerse cattle for $18 a head, with the spring calves included. The cattle were to be paid for with fat beef cattle rounded up, counted, and branded. A brand with the letters *D R* was adopted to represent Daggett Ranch. The place was everywhere known as the Van Dyke Ranch.* This irritated the Funks. They vainly tried to educate the public to call it something different. Bill Boreham, the blacksmith who made the branding iron, derisively remarked that it stood for Damned Robbers.

Bill was no saint. A schoolteacher, perceiving him peeping in her window, fired a shot at him. His footsteps indicated that he had raced off at high speed.

Having raised cattle on an Indiana farm, Mr. Funk deemed himself an authority on range cattle. Buel, ambitious to be a hero on horseback, adorned himself with cowboy regalia. Dix brought nothing. To him, chasing cattle was just another chore, one that had to be learned.

Some of the cattle were quite wild, some tame enough to be stubborn. None were easy to drive. The crew raced the wild ones and lashed the stubborn ones with rawhide whips until most of them were gathered. There were less than one hundred head. Someone had stolen part of the herd. Some people furtively accused Jack Le Furgey of butchering and selling them, but he could not have used so many. Where they went remained a mystery.

Good rains made the bunch grass green. Miles of grass grew along the uplands adjacent to the river, and the ranchers estimated the range

---

*It is still known as this or as the Old Van Dyke Ranch, though the sign to the entrance bears the more recent name Coolwater Ranch.

would support 1,000 head of cattle. They were yet to learn of dry years, when no rain fell and the galleta grass that now waved in the breeze would be as nourishing as an old broom.

Again grass and flowers flourished across the desert, and the ranch had a good rabbit crop. They were not as numerous as during the past year, but with the advent of June they congregated about the ranch and again began making holes in the fence. The ranchers stopped this by hanging an eighteen-inch strip of chicken netting around the outside of the fence and sprawling the lower edge out on the ground. The rabbits could get between the two rows of netting but would not make a hole through the inner one. Maybe they did not like the outer one banging them on the tail while they worked.

19

FISH HORNS AT A WILD ROUNDUP ◆ BUEL FUNK SPARKS HELEN MUIR ◆ AN EMBARRASSING WEDDING NIGHT ◆ MR. FUNK'S FOOLISHNESS ◆ In July Jack Le Furgey decided to remove to Nevada, and he sold his cattle to the ranch for $20 a head, with yearling calves included. It was a better buy than the Ryerse cattle. Frank Ryerse loaned the purchase price and agreed to accept fat cattle in payment.

"Be sure and draw up an airtight bill of sale and include the whole family," Dix admonished the Judge.

He did, and the bill of sale delivered ownership of the cattle when signed by Jack, his wife, and two daughters before the roundup began. Rounding up these cattle was a tough job.

Many thousands of years ago, the lower end of the Silver Valley was a great lake fed by the Mojave River, which was then a large stream. The river finally broke through the barrier hills, cutting the Caves Canyon, and poured into the deep rift of which Death Valley forms the northern portion. Then the river began scouring a channel upstream through the valley. In time the increasing aridity of the climate ended the scouring, and the river has ever since had the peculiarity of a channel that increased in steepness of grade as the river descended. At Camp Cady the channel was seventy feet below the floor of the valley.

Normally dry for most of its length, here the river flows for a distance of six miles, fed by underground water in the area. The upper four miles contain a dense thicket of mesquite a quarter of a mile wide, so thick in places that it is difficult to lead a horse through. The lower two miles have open places and grassy meadows.

Here, Frank Parish lived a solitary life for seventeen years, during which he built miles of fences constructed of poles fastened to posts with discarded baling wire. He grubbed trees and brush off the meadows and leveled them. He constructed a log house and a stable and also a great barn of logs in which his herd of cattle could seek refuge from the flies during the summer. There was a large black fly resembling a bumblebee and a small gray one that would stick tight to a horse and not fly when one's hand descended upon it. Also a small black fly that clustered upon the cattle's shoulders beyond the reach of their tails, plus clouds of small gnats that caused the riders to wear handkerchiefs tucked under their hats and draped about their necks. Some rubbed kerosene about their shirts to repel the flies. All told, they were a summer curse that drove all the cattle into the thickets, where they remained during the day. Because of the flies, the range horses stayed far from the river during the daytime and ventured in to drink only at night.

During the first roundup in April, the cattle were grazing on bunch grass and flowers far from the river. There they were easily gathered. Now they were in the thickets.

Le Furgey's ranch was four miles from the upper end of the thickets, and there he butchered cattle. It was his custom to seek a bunch of cattle grazing outside of the mesquites, rush upon them with a whooping and yelling, and start them running away from the brush and toward his ranch. As he progressed toward home, he would drop out those he did not want. His method resulted in making some of the cattle wild as deer and causing the tame ones to be difficult to drive. The wild cattle would not venture from the brush except at dusk, and they returned before sunup.

The roundup crew was a motley group. Le Furgey and his girls rode astride; his wife, a fine rider, used a sidesaddle. She had learned that way and never became accustomed to riding like a man. With them was a gawky railway employee and a fourteen-year-old boy. Both worked for nothing because they were enamored with the oldest daughter. The Van Dyke ranch crowd was not much better. Dix had a rawhide riata, and Buel sported a small popgun, riding boots, and some fancy duds. No one had a trained roping horse, knew how to handle one, or could lasso anything from the back of a running horse. It was a poor gang to pursue wild cattle.

Dix conceived the bright idea of securing a dozen tin fish horns, such as kids delight to blow on a New Year's Eve. The gang strung out in a row, all armed with horns and leading their saddlehorses. They wended their way through the thickets, making a discordant din from which the cattle fled. At the upper end they scattered in every direction. Some were easily driven, but the wild ones turned at bay before running far. It was midsummer and the weather intensely hot. In such high temperatures cattle soon become overheated and if wild will usually turn and fight. Mr. Le Furgey's railroad helper emptied a revolver at one but failed to hit it. Most of the wild ones regained the thickets, but a few were driven into the corral at Le Furgey's ranch. One wild cow chased everyone from the corral, and she was left overnight to cool off. In the morning she was dead, killed by overheating.

The fish horns worked fine for three days. By that time the wild cattle had learned that men and not Devils were making the terrible racket, and they could not be driven out. However, most of the cattle were gathered and branded. All had to be lassoed, dragged to a snubbing post, and thrown down. Then they were stretched out by a rope looped about the hind legs and held by a saddlehorse. They all got up fighting, and each time the men on foot doing the branding had to take refuge on the fence until they were driven away by the horsemen.

It was hard, hot work, and everyone became cranky and irritable and indulged in caustic remarks. Le Furgey's son-in-law and Buel displayed cautious natures. Dix and Old Jack did most of the footwork. This irritated Mrs. Le Furgey.

"John and Dix," she bawled, "are you the only brave men in the crowd? Everyone else is afraid."

This reacted on Mr. Funk, who with Mrs. Le Furgey was keeping tally of the cattle. He made some nasty remarks to his offspring and invited him to change places with him. The spectators snickered with joy, and Buel sullenly refused.

Yet most of the cattle were branded and paid for, and the Le Furgeys left. Jack said he would return in the fall and help gather the remnant and some range horses that had been sold with the cattle. He never did.

The ranchers now possessed more than 200 head of range cattle with a free range. The cattle had been bought cheap, and everyone felt quite cheerful. The hay market was beginning to look dubious. The new borax mine on the east end of the Calicos quit operations after investing a large sum of money, and there was little teaming to do. There was some sale of hay to the new settlers, but they were grading land and threatening to produce more hay and flood the market. There was plenty of range feed and enough watering places along the river. The cattle required little care during warm weather.

The Van Dykes had plenty of water for irrigating, and the hay crops were good.

In August a large stack of baled hay stood near the edge of a wide, shallow swale that traversed the ranch. The hay was laid on boards and on land deemed safe from any moisture. The desert has a summer rainy season, but there had not yet been anything but a light shower on the ranch in summertime. Then one day the weather began to cool and get cloudy, and there were distant rolls of thunder. The like had often been seen before, and work went on as usual.

By noon, a dark curtain obscured the hills three miles south of the ranch.

"Hugh," observed Dix, "that looks like a cloudburst up there, a solid sheet of water falling. I am going to saddle a horse and ride up along the ditch and see about damage."

Before he could secure the horse, the deluge struck the ranch with hailstones the size of marbles pelting down. Dix led his trembling horse into the blacksmith shop and waited. The storm lasted only half an hour, but three inches of rain fell and much more on the higher slopes where the storm began.

Dix rode off toward town. A few small streams crossed the road, and the storm seemed a trivial affair, but the torrents came after he passed, pouring down from the mountain slopes above. In various places they flowed over the railroad tracks, and they filled the canal with soft mud and debris. The swale through the ranch became a river. Water stood a foot deep about the haystack, and in a hog pen on higher ground the swine had to swim until rescued. The growing crops just ready to harvest were beaten flat to the ground. All hands immediately began work on the canal. They spent more than two weeks of arduous labor to remove the mud and debris and allow irrigation water to reach the parched crops. At this time of year they needed irrigating every ten days.

The Van Dykes estimated the total damage at $1,500, an amount that exceeded the year's profits. Farmers must expect occasional calamities, and most of them are fatalistic about such matters. There were many vituperative remarks but little repining.

For a year Buel had been sparking Miss Muir. No one paid much attention because of the disparity in their ages, and during most of the time Buel had been attending high school on the Coast.* Now he went to Los Angeles for some ostensible purpose. Three days later, the lady followed. Maybe she felt foolish about it. She left in the night, and her future pappy-in-law escorted her to Yermo, where she thought she could board a train unobserved by acquaintances. Much to her disgust, a Daggett lad was the night baggage agent.

The marriage was performed the next day in Los Angeles. The couple began their honeymoon there in the Van Nuys Hotel, which had rules that might now be regarded as puritanical.† Buel lingered at

---

*Some years later, the census of 1920 for Daggett gave Buel's age as thirty, Helen's as thirty-three. By then, the couple had four sons.

†Cowboy Buel was trying to impress his new bride. Workman notes the international reputation of the Van Nuys Hotel and comments that "its cuisine and service were

the desk to register while the bride proceeded to the elevator flanked by bellboys carrying the luggage. As Buel turned from the desk, the clerk, who knew him and had observed the lady's age, leaned over the desk and chillingly inquired,

"Say, Buel, what are you trying to do? Don't you know any better than to try that here?"

A local paper printed a flamboyant announcement of the wedding. One of Buel's schoolmates coached the reporter. He described Buel as a cowboy and an artist—the latter because of some amateur paintings he had done. This produced much merriment in Daggett, and long thereafter Buel was referred to as the cowboy artist.

The natives tried to get a rise out of Dix by jeering at his lack of acumen in not trying to grab a wealthy bride, but he did not care. He was still expecting to be enriched by the ranch, and he did not possess a sordid nature. Amusements were scarce, and joking and raillery relieved the monotony of things.

Mr. Hugh Funk added to the gaiety of things by a foolish exploit which caused him some humiliation and which might have been expected from a tenderfoot but not from one who deemed himself an authority on cattle.

The railways required a caretaker to accompany cars of cattle, and he acted as such for a car of cattle that the local butcher bought far out on the desert. At Daggett there was no pen, only a chute for unloading cattle. The car arrived in the night and was shunted beside the chute.

There were thirty-five head of weary cattle in the car, and Mr. Funk conceived the bright idea of opening the car door so they could venture out and lie down on mother earth. Then he went home and to bed.

When he returned in the morning, there were yet twenty-four head near the car, but the others all had disappeared. He and Buel spent several hours in futile search and were jeeringly informed by the

known throughout the world. Royalty and famous folk without number inscribed their names on its register. When President and Mrs. William McKinley came here in 1901, they made their headquarters at the Van Nuys" (350).

cattle's owner that they should send for Dix. He would know enough to follow the cattle's tracks instead of riding about with his head in the air.

A cowboy traveling with two horses arrived in the village that evening, and his services were enlisted. He tracked one steer twenty-five miles, lassoed it, and tied it to a bush. Later, it was hauled back in a wagon. Several escaped into the mesquite thickets and were eventually gathered in future roundups.

During the previous winter the ranchers had begun driving a water tunnel under the river from the head of the great canal. This was slow work. They drove redwood planks four feet long, two inches thick, and six inches wide with a sledgehammer. They shoveled the dirt backward and inserted side and roof braces of redwood six inches square. The work was again resumed with the advent of winter. It was done at that time because there was little work on the ranch except land grading. Fortunately, Dix was too tall to work in the tunnel and was using a team for some levee work.

A large flood had not come down the river in eighteen years. It was not then possible to get accurate information about the snow in the mountain watershed, and the ranchers had no premonition of impending disaster. The cookhouse was down in the big canal. Dix, who slept outdoors beside the house, was awakened before dawn on New Year's Day by a roaring noise and quickly learned it was caused by a great torrent flowing down the river.

Heavy snows up in the mountains, followed by a thaw and rain, caused the deluge. Dix went into the tunnel to board up the face of it and found it rather terrifying. Water was pouring in from both roof and sides, and an occasional gush of water sounded like the collapse of the roof. He did not like it but remained until he finished the job.

There was a dirt dam across the head of the canal, and a wing dam extended out into the river channel. The water kept rising, and all hands began working on the dam. With a team Dix dragged dirt onto it, and with shovels the others kept heaping it up as high as possible. At times the water poured over places in the dam, and the shovelers despairingly declared there was no hope of raising the dam fast enough.

"We ain't going to quit until we have to," declared Dix.

As the flood increased, the end of the wing dam kept cutting away. By midday the wing dam was gone, but the river was rapidly falling. The dam lasted long enough to save the canal.

The next day snow began falling. It was a welcomed sight, for there could be no more floods until warmer weather. The flood destroyed the five railway bridges on the river, and the same weather conditions produced destructive floods in Nevada that caused the suspension of all traffic on the Salt Lake Railway for a whole year. Repairs cost the railway company two million dollars.

20 "AN INCURABLE FASCINATION" ♦ FAT ETTA ♦ BITTERNESS WITH FUNK ♦ THE ROMANCE OF RANGE CATTLE ♦ The ranchers abandoned the tunnel work and never resumed it. Driving the tunnel was too difficult and costly. In later years, they learned that a tunnel had been begun several hundred feet downstream from the submerged reef that crossed the river. This never would have produced very much water.

The ranchers now had sixty acres producing alfalfa, and they felt sure that when they had one hundred acres there would be sufficient income to pay expenses. The funds provided by Funk and Kerckhoff had been exhausted, and the ranchers depended on credit from the Ryerse store to carry on. Dix and Hugh Funk had each received $900 in salary during the first year after Mr. Funk's coming, but they had agreed to depend upon profits for any future payments. Dix now had six years' wages to his credit.

Daggett was a moribund town. The successors of Old Mike closed the saloon and left. Alex remained. He had accumulated enough wealth and had lived too long in Daggett to move elsewhere. He continued to operate his saloon in a desultory manner, but now few came to blow a stake. One restaurant remained. Old Antone had closed his and returned to China to run a peanut stand on the streets of Hong

Kong. The Hillis store carried only a small stock of goods. Hillis didn't have enough to make it profitable for his creditors to foreclose, and he was too stubborn to voluntarily file a petition in bankruptcy. By a strange quirk, the cloudburst of the previous year saved him. The railway decided to build storm ditches to prevent any future damage, and Hillis secured the contract at a very profitable figure. The work was all close to home, and he was able to secure enough horses and scrapers to do the work. In those days expensive machinery for moving dirt was yet to be invented.

There seemed to be an incurable fascination about the squalid little town that caused the dwellers to linger and leave reluctantly. Some of those who left to seek employment elsewhere occasionally returned and stayed for a while. Some had never earned a dollar in Daggett, but it was yet home to them. A few moved to Barstow and Yermo.

After futile attempts to sell his livery stable, Byron Rowan left, but in a year he returned and for a time operated it. Joe Goodrich, the master mechanic of the borax company, went to the Death Valley mines, but in a year he, too, returned and continued to dwell in Daggett for the remainder of his life. One of the demimondaine remained: Fat Etta. She was a domestic creature who showed evidence of Indian and Jewish ancestry. She owned her own house, never drank or smoked, and seemed content with a quiet life and few visitors. In later years she adopted an abandoned female Mexican baby and cared for her like a real mother until the girl was respectably married. Etta gave up her profession before the girl became old enough to learn anything about it.

Many of the old miners who had made the town a rendezvous had died. A few depended upon a monthly dole of $10 from the county. These were the solicitude of Seymour Alf, who was the road foreman for the district. Occasionally, he gave them a few days' work on the road. It was illegal to hire paupers on the dole, but Alf was a sterling character known to be incapable of committing any shady transaction for his own gain, and the practice was ignored. The old miners were a pathetic class. When they became too old to toil in the mines, most of them seemed unable to gain a livelihood.

The Pepper Tree Club dwindled. A fire destroyed Alex's saloon, and he moved his bar into the old dancehall across the street. Occasionally, a dance was held in the railway freight station or the schoolhouse. There, annual picnics and a community Xmas tree continued. At times there was a ballgame when a team came over from Yermo with a switch engine and a freight car for transportation. This was a violation of some rule or law, but the railway officials ignored it until some grouch filed a formal complaint, and they had to forbid it.

The old, free and easy ways were passing. It had begun with the suppression of vice, and Fred Johnson followed with the suppression of noisy drunks. He had not had an easy time of it. Of course, a drunken hobo could be summarily dealt with, but when one of the natives became a nuisance, both Constable and Judge endeavored to wean him from his habit without resorting to a jail sentence.

Shorty Harris and Shorty Marian were boon companions when sober, and both got drunk together. When locked in jail together, they fought. If one was turned out, he was drunk before the other became sober. Harris finally deserted the town, and Marian got another chum. One day the Constable brought Shorty before the Judge for another scolding.

When he was leaving, Dix said, "Shorty, don't ever come here again. The next time it will be ninety days."

"Aw, the Judge won't do that," he replied.

"I know the Judge. You have been here enough. Don't come again," answered Dix.

The next day the Constable brought the chum. He tearfully promised to leave the town and cause no more disturbance and was allowed to go. Before the day ended, he was again drunk and facing the Judge.

"Ninety days in jail," rasped the Judge.

Shorty Marian was drinking in the saloon when he heard the direful news coupled with the information that the Constable was seeking him. Shorty started down the street going west, and it was twenty years before he again visited Daggett.

Dieterle sold his interest to Kerckhoff, Van Dyke, and Funk. They agreed to pay him $500 each year for twenty years, and he retained a loan on his interest for the unpaid installments. He had contributed no money to the enterprise but was eloquent in discoursing about the value of his "services" rendered over a period of years while living in Los Angeles and engaged in other occupations. The Judge and Dix each had a Desert Land entry of 320 acres adjoining the original ranch. Dix was but an employee, but he represented the Judge's interest and also that of Kerckhoff. This irked the Funks. They did not believe that Dix should be allowed a voice in the management of the ranch.

The Judge had deeded to Dix a water right for eighty inches of water to enable him to gain title to his land. This allowed Funk's relatives an opportunity to work on his credulity and convince him that it was a fraudulent scheme to deprive him of a share of his water. Funk was too ignorant to know that the Judge could deed nothing except a portion of his own share. Dieterle also had a Desert Land entry, and Funk paid him $500 for it. Forty acres of the Judge's land had been graded and planted to alfalfa and was now producing.

The government land office issued patents upon Desert Land entries when one eighth of the acreage was planted to irrigated crops and some other formalities were completed. When the Judge endeavored to make his final proof and secure title to the land, he was informed that a new ruling from Washington had ordained that every acre must be properly graded and planted to irrigated crops. There was only one recourse. He abandoned half of his acreage and filed a homestead on the remainder. Then to get title, he had to build a cabin on the land and sleep there each night. Fortunately, he did not have to eat there. Sleeping fulfilled the duty of making it "his home." The Judge continued this routine for five years to secure title to the land.

Dix was in a quandary. He had not yet planted alfalfa but was preparing to. He filed a homestead entry on half of his land, erected a cabin on it, and emulated his father. He had a mile to travel and used a horse. Dix was not an owner in the irrigation system. This enabled him to make a plea for an extension of time for the filing of proof upon the remainder of his desert entry. He represented that he had in good faith purchased a water right, and the sellers had failed to deliver the water in time to enable him to comply with the legal requirements of the government. He was allowed two years additional time. He did not know what good it would do him, but he believed in never giving up until necessary. Two years later, some of the Funk retainers secured a copy of his petition and boasted that they would secure his conviction for perjury. Nothing came of it. The petition contained only true facts. There had not been sufficient water, and Dix had worked too long on the Judge's land for anyone to prove he had not bought the water rights.

The year 1910 began favorably. Though powerful, the flood did no damage. Dix had excavated a long ditch on the opposite side of the river and the flood widened it. In time the ditch diverted the floods away from the canal. He had done the work alone. Funk bitterly opposed this, declaring that water would not flow through the ditch. Dix also dug a shallow ditch in the river's channel to gather the water forced to the surface by the submerged reef. There was plenty of water for all of the alfalfa fields. Plenty of feed grew on the cattle range, and, fortunately, the flood had come in the night when the cattle were grazing away from the riverbottom. At Camp Cady the flood cut a path 600 feet wide through the mesquite thickets, taking out all the trees.

Twelve years before, a cattle herd being driven through the country had brought Texas ticks. These spread Texas fever, and many cattle died. The survivors bred immune descendants. The disease started in Texas, and cattle taken from there to other states spread ruin among the native herds. Until recent years, people derided the idea that the fever was spread by ticks. Now the government was trying to cleanse California of ticks by confining cattle in pastures where they could be frequently dipped until the ticks were eradicated. This year the authorities began at Camp Cady.

Again Dix had to round up his cattle, confine them in a pasture, and plunge them into a deep vat dug in the ground. Yet it was impossible to gather a small bunch that hid in the mesquite thickets. Those wild cattle would come out only at night and must be gathered at dusk and dawn. Some would run like horses, others turned and dodged past the rider and back into the thickets. In places there were small sand hills covered with a thick growth of mesquite brush. Some of the critters would dart in there and crouch down like rabbits. A horse couldn't penetrate that mess, and Dix had no trained dog to chase them out. Dix left them there and drove the rest of the cattle to a new desert range at Soda Lake.

A lot of drivel has been written about the romance of handling range cattle. The best that can be said for cowboying is that it is not monotonous and is sometimes exciting and even entertaining. But it is not a job for softies, and a timid person will gather few cattle where they are wild and the ground rough. A cowboy has to pursue them at breakneck speeds without fear of stumbling or being knocked out of the saddle by overhanging limbs. He must expect accidents, but not fear them.

21 THE PROPHET ELIJAH DISCOURSES ON DAGGETT ♦ A CATTLE DRIVE TO SODA LAKE ♦ DIX OVERWHELMED BY AWE ♦ AN OLD MAN AND A ONE-ARMED BOY ♦ One day the gang was gathering cattle near Le Furgey's ranch and tarried there for lunch. The caretaker was an old pioneer named Issac Bateman. For many years he lived in a ruined abode. He claimed to be the reincarnation of the Prophet Elijah, and he was in constant communication with Celestial Visitors who frequently called in the stillness of the night.

Doctor Mc Farlane dubbed him insane and declared him to be a paranoiac. Others opined that too much whiskey imbibed in his youth had addled his wits. However, Issac could talk sensibly enough upon various subjects, that is, until someone enquired whether he did not become lonely living by himself. Whereupon, Issac regaled his visitors with fantastic tales.

This day he was beguiled into telling how he had visited the graveyard at Kernville to ascertain how many people there had gone to Heaven. It had been a tough mining town where long before many men had died with their boots on.

"There was just a few children. That was all," he mournfully related.

"Mr. Bateman," asked Dix, "did you ever inspect the graveyard at Daggett to see how many have gone to Heaven?"

The old man looked very gloomy, and in most solemn tones said, "Yes, I have been up there, and I've looked them all over, and they ain't nary a one."

Bill Frakes was the sole inhabitant at Cady. He gradually accumulated several hundred sheep that were immune to local diseases. He'd started out determined to crossbreed the wild desert sheep with domestic breeds. He caught the wild sheep by placing steel traps in the trails where they came to water and then patiently watched the trap until a victim was caught.

The first two he captured Bill sold to the government for a zoo. During a period of years, he caught about twenty wild sheep, but he never secured a cross. Some of the bighorns were too wild and were averse to the tame sheep. Most of them died in captivity, and no one else has ever succeeded in doing what he attempted. Probably the two breeds are not near enough akin. Wild sheep fight off coyotes, and he hoped to get a crossbreed that would do the same and not need protection.

Driving the cattle to Soda Lake was an onerous task. It was a mixed herd with many old cows and young calves. Many were refractory and none trained to drive. Among them were sixty head of tame cattle raised by old Frank Parish within a pasture. The latter required much lashing with leather whips to keep them in the herd. Twenty miles had to be traversed the first day. The drive began at 3 A.M. and ended at midnight in the Afton Canyon where it was narrowest. There, camp could be made and the cattle prevented from returning.

The following day the cattle rested while the crew gathered posts and built a drift fence across the canyon to prevent the cattle from returning to Cady. The homing instinct is ever strong, and, regardless of the enticements of a new range, cattle always try to return to their old home. The canyon had been scoured by the river through a range of hills. For a distance of five miles the walls were too steep for cattle to climb, and here the canyon formed a natural pocket for them to gather in. Upstream from the canyon the underground water of the river came to the surface and flowed on top for a long distance. It is a place of great natural beauty, but the cow whackers were too tired to enjoy the scenery. The flood of the preceding January had destroyed the three bridges in the canyon and strewn the wreckage though it. It was well for the cattle that no trains were to pass through during the balance of the year.

The third day's drive was easier and ended near Soda Lake. This was really the southern part of the great rift valley, the northern part of which is called Death Valley. Here the river ended, and the flood waters spread over a great dry lake bed and flowed yet farther into Silver Lake, where the water was confined. Below the canyon, some of the flood water flowed through a gap in the hills into Cronise Lake and at times formed a large body of water. Soda Lake and vicinity appeared to be a basin surrounded by ranges of desert hills and mountains. In reality it was merely a wide place in the deep wrinkle extending for 200 miles across the desert. The lake bed was 900 feet above sea level, four miles wide, and ten long. Long ago, the Mojave River broke into the basin and formed a lake thirty miles long. Archaeologists prowling about its ancient beach lines have found rude tools fashioned from chipped stones.

Where the river debouched into the lake bed, there was a large area of alluvial soil with underground water close to the surface. In places, scant growths of mesquite trees, salt grass, and brush grew on level flats. There was also a large area of sandy land with small sand hills scattered about. Much of this maintained a heavy growth of wild millet that was now in seed. It was a desert plant, but it was new to this locality, and old-timers who had known the land long before knew nothing of it. There was plenty of feed for the cattle, and their owners thought there would be little trouble caring for them.

Far to the east and north towering ranges marked the horizon, while from the great heights extending downward into the deep sink were ranges of hills and smaller mountains not deemed worth bestowing names upon. The whole landscape formed a vast panorama that created a feeling of awe.

The Salt Lake Railway crossed the basin at the north end of Soda Lake and climbed the long mountain slope to the east. The Tonopah and Tidewater passed along the westerly side, bound for the mining camps of Nevada. The trains were to cause the deaths of some cattle, but they also made the shipping of supplies easy. The building of the railway a few years before caused an influx of homesteaders, but they were now all gone, leaving a few ruined habitations and a two-story hotel some optimistic dupe had built and abandoned. More abandoned homesteads were beyond the north end of the lake, and around Cronise Lake a few hopeful souls yet lingered. Most of the homesteaders had been beguiled by land locators who secured a fat fee for locating them and had painted the prospects in rosy hues. The same had happened and was yet to occur again in various places in the great desert.

A few years before, an old man with a one-armed boy arrived in Daggett driving a decrepit old horse hitched to a rickety wagon and bound for Death Valley and the rich lands a locator had glowingly described. The local residents persuaded him to go no farther, telling him that while he might get there, it was certain that the old horse would not be able to bring him back.

The mental processes that have induced people to settle upon worthless desert lands is a puzzle that no one has ever been able to analyze. They could not be induced to buy the land outright for even a trivial sum. Even when after they have acquired title by much expense and hardship, they can rarely find a buyer, and they desert the land. Even then, those who would not buy from them will locate on even more worthless land in the same locality and endure the same distressing experiences. They seem to be obsessed with the belief that they are going to get something for nothing. That the government is giving it to them free of costs. Most of them with grim determination maintain a residence until they can make final proof and secure a patent from the land office, and then they immediately abandon the place.

A cow camp was established beneath some spreading mesquite trees. There were several shallow pools of water, plenty of green feed, and Lou, the cowboy, termed it a Cow Heaven. The cows had different ideas. The homing instinct was strong in them, and they pined for the thickets in the Cady riverbottom. Each night a band would start for home, and each morning riders hastened after them and drove them back. The fence across the canyon stopped them, and they soon learned to drive so well that one man could drive a large herd back. However, the calves could not be branded or gelded because they could not withstand the additional hardship it would cause.

Buel and his wife helped to drive the cattle, and together with Dix they tarried for a while, and then Lou was left alone with the cattle. The cattle still hankered for their old home but did not venture off in other directions.

The Van Dykes harvested a good hay crop on the ranch and graded more land for fall planting. Buel retired from hard work and prevailed upon his father to furnish the money for buying an interest in an advertising agency in Los Angeles. He and his wife moved there. It was the last money the old man had left from the sale of his property near Los Angeles, and he never got it back.

Business conditions on the desert were moribund. Mining was dead and was to stay so for a long time. The old prospectors, together with the native Indians, were a vanishing race. The old roamers of the desert were all part of a passing era. The boom mining camps of southern Nevada had flourished for a time, but some were already abandoned and others dwindling. Rhyolite now had only six inhabitants, where once there had once been thousands. The Tonopah and Tidewater Railway, built with great expectations, now depended upon the borax mines at Death Valley for enough freight to partially pay expenses. Interest on their bonds was never paid. The Las Vegas and Goldfield Railway was abandoned, and the rails torn up and used elsewhere. The little freighting with teams that yet survived thrived on hauling abandoned mining machinery to the railways, which shipped it to junkyards far away. A few miners lingered about the abandoned camps, clinging to their claims and hoping for a revival.

Silver Lake was as far as the flood waters of the Mojave River ever got. A village had sprung up beside it. This had stores, saloons, a jail, a constable, and a justice of the peace. It dwindled to four old miners and a railway agent, and finally only the agent remained.

22 HERONYMOUS HARTMAN SHOT DEAD ♦ MONSTER FLIES AND SOME HARDSCRABBLE PEOPLE ♦ DIX'S GIFT ♦ THE JUDGE AND JOHN MUIR ♦ MISS MARY BEAL ♦ Farther up the river at Oro Grande, a brief revival of the frontier days ended tragically. Heronymous Hartman was an elderly German who long before had been a soldier at Camp Cady. Later he became a rancher and cattleman upon the riverbottom. He had many years before killed a renegade negro for whom a reward had been offered. The negro was hiding in the riverbottom thickets, thinking that he could trust Hartman.

Since then, Hartman had been in some rows and shooting scrapes. He married a woman who deserted him, and without the formality of a divorce he married another woman. He served two years in prison for this escapade, but wife number two remained true to him and cared for the ranch and cattle during his absence. Then, in a drunken rage he shot at his stepdaughter with a rifle. He was convicted on a felony charge and was at liberty under bonds. Early on the day of his sentencing, he got on another drunken rampage in the village of Oro Grande, where he resided.

The Justice of the Peace there was a young man who later testified that he had been elected because he was the only inhabitant who was not afraid of Hartman. When the Judge appeared on the scene with a club in his hand, Hartman ran for his house with the Judge after him. Naturally, the Judge supposed he was seeking a gun and shot him dead on the steps of his dwelling.

There was much condemnation of the Judge and many praises of Hartman's reputation for virtue.

"It beats the deuce," commented Mr. Jack Duane, "on how people change. I knew Hartman for twenty-five years and never heard a good word spoken for him until he was dead."

Hartman's widow paid a lawyer $500 to prosecute the Judge, who had been arrested and jailed. He was soon freed on bonds and acquitted at a preliminary trial.

The railway performed much construction work at Barstow, building new tracks, making cuts and fills, and erecting a large hotel and depot, together with a clubhouse for employees.* It brought many laborers and attracted some criminals. For a time the town was tough, but nothing like Daggett had been. Railroad officers dispersed the inhabitants of some brothels that had long existed in the riverbottom, and after that order was fairly maintained.

A bunch of wild cattle was still taking refuge in the dense thickets at the upper end of the Cady brush. Dix fenced the one waterhole there to compel the cattle to seek water elsewhere. Before the job was completed, word came from Soda Lake that the waterholes there were drying up, and someone must be sent to deepen them. Dix had to go. He deepened the holes with a team and scraper. For the first time he found hot weather tiring and frequently rested in the shade. He knew the midsummer temperature was high, but the effects puzzled him. He learned it was due to the humidity that had caused several deaths elsewhere on the desert. During this time, a passenger got off a train and lay down in the shade of the abandoned hotel. Later he was found dead. He was a miner who had come from the Coast and was soaked in whiskey. The booze and heat had been too much for his heart.

One cloudless day at Soda Lake a muddy stream of flood water came down the river channel. Dix didn't solve the mystery until he returned to Cady, where a great cloudburst had deluged the locality. Several inches of rain fell in a short time. The flood washed away part of the drift fence in the canyon. On his way home, Dix tried to repair it, but horseflies large as bumblebees made him quit. They would light

---

*Given his aversion to high society, Dix may never have entered this lavish hotel and restaurant complex run by Fred Harvey. A great, gracious, multistoried expanse of a building built in the pseudo Spanish-Moroccan style, with turrets and arches, the Casa Del Desierto, opened in 1911, filled the residents of humble Barstow with awe. Says Germaine L. Moon, "It was almost a self-contained little city, and the fifth luxurious edifice built west of Albuquerque" (13). Casa Del Desierto still stands out there, a crumbling fantasy looming on the desert. It is in the process of being restored.

on his back and jab through his thin shirt. The job required another man to fight flies while one worked. For some reason the flies were very plentiful there. Because the rain left numerous pools of water about Cady, Dix temporarily abandoned his efforts to gather the wild cattle.

Bill Frakes was an expert tracker. He boasted that no man could evade him once he was on his trail. He allowed his sheep to wander about without herding and depended on his skill as a trapper to catch any wildcats or coyotes that preyed on them. He would circle the riverbottom and detect the track of any newcomer, animal or human, to his realm. He could also easily distinguish the foottracks of those he knew by their manner of walking. Some Mexican section hands living on the railway three miles away annoyed him by stealing trifling amounts of flour and sugar from his house. They believed the thefts would not be noticed. They were.

One day Frakes paid them a visit. He knocked one down with his huge revolver and pointed it at another while he plied a lash about his body, meanwhile vowing that he would kill the next Mexican he encountered in the riverbottom. That night the whole crew decamped, and the railway had to hire a new gang.

"I never steal from anybody," he declared, "and when anyone steals from me it makes me mad and I want to kill them."

Camp Cady once was an Army fort embracing 1,800 acres, but years ago the military abandoned it. The present dwellers there had squatted on portions of it. Through some connivance by those in authority, the Southern Pacific Railway Company secured title to a square mile of it as part of the government land grants given them for building the railway. This land included the places fenced and built by Old Swanze and Frank Parish, and Dix leased them from the railway. The deal gave him exclusive possession of some large, enclosed pastures. Dix also purchased the Parish cattle and added them to his other herds.

Parish returned and was again dwelling in his log house. Dix said nothing to him about the lease and established his headquarters on the Swanze place. Parish was a mean, cantankerous old curmudgeon, and when he learned through others of the lease, he abandoned the place. Two newcomers squatted in the riverbottom. Their arrival perturbed Mr. Funk, who now believed he had a vested interest in the free range. However, Dix was not concerned and quickly became chummy with them. The desert was plenty big. Why try to hog it?

R. H. Woods was the survivor of a vanishing type. He possessed a wife, a ten-year-old son, a gun, some traps, and about twenty small, runty Indian mustangs. Nonetheless, he deemed himself a man of substance. The family lived like Indians, cared nothing about discomforts or privations, and were content with the most meager fare.

"The trouble with these California people," quoth Mr. Woods, "is that they are so used to having money that they think they can't get along without it. I kin because I ain't used to having it." He had been raised in Arkansas.

George Willis was a remainder from the mining boom. For a year he and his wife lived in Daggett, and with the other promoters he dug imaginary holes in the sidewalk between the saloons and talked glowingly of his rich prospects, or rather, "mines," as he termed them. No one believed there was any worth in them. Then the Willises squatted on some damp land and were trying to raise food in a small garden. They were poorer than Woods, for they possessed no livestock. They seemed quite happy and content and never wailed about their fate.

"Don't those two beat Hell?" commented Mr. Frakes. "Whenever they are together they act like they just got married."

They continued to act that way until George died seventeen years later. Dix enriched them with the gift of a saddlehorse. It was not worth much, but it doubled their wealth, and they always gratefully remembered the gift. The horse enabled George to earn some money grubbing brush on desert land claims far from his camp.

The Judge was getting old, but his health remained good. He no longer wrote for publications but continued to paint pictures and daily pored over his beloved tomes of ancient Greek and Latin. Occasionally he toiled in his small vegetable garden or walked to the village, where he drank beer and conversed with the few old men who doddered about. They respected his learning and regarded him with esteem, but they were not his kind, and he hungered for intellectual companionship.

Because of this, he was delighted when John Muir paid a visit to the ranch. Then the two spent much time together. They found each other congenial souls and never disagreed on any subject.

Not so the Judge's brother. He arrived during one of Muir's visits, and the two wrangled incessantly about various highbrowed topics. Then Muir came no more, and the brother's visits were far apart.* The Judge never complained. He had adopted a philosophy that nothing mattered much. He gave little concern to the management of ranch affairs, except at long intervals when he bestowed some caustic remarks upon his son. Dix cared nothing for that. He knew that his father's love for him had ever been strong, and his love for his father was too great to allow anything—even a woman—to come between them.

Two newcomers arrived at the ranch. One was a young lady, Miss Mary Beal, who came for her health. She pitched a tent beneath a cottonwood tree and began a temporary residence that continued until she became known as an old inhabitant. She was a highbrowed gal who dabbled in literature, astronomy, ornithology, and botany. In time she became quite expert in those things.†

The other was a young man named Ray Clifford. He was well bred and well educated. He talked book language. That irked the Funks and their retainers, but Dix liked Clifford and often took him along on his trips over the cattle range.

With the advent of cool weather, Dix prepared to round up the bunch of wild cattle and bargained for a dog trained to chase cattle from thickets. Mr. Funk bestowed upon Dix much detailed and exact information on the proper procedure for gathering the cattle. This irked Dix, and he told Funk to gather the cattle himself, and he would

---

*In contrast to the conflict Dix describes, in his autobiography name-dropping John C. Van Dyke writes breezily pleasant memories of Muir (167–68). In fact, Van Dyke claims that he was "much flattered by [Muir] saying in his simple Scotch way that he had made this trip, at this time, that he might meet me" (167).

†The Epilogue has more to say about this lively and unusual pioneer of desert botany.

work on the ranch. As a result, Dix spent the winter grading land upon his desert claim. By the spring he had twenty-two acres of growing alfalfa. Mr. Funk, with the aid of three or four men, spent a month gathering thirty head of wild cattle. Funk and his men would return to the ranch after a week's futile effort, looking like a picture of Napoleon's Retreat from Moscow.

"It's Hell," said Mr. Funk.

He eventually solved the problem by arming the crew with shotguns and shooting the cattle on sight with birdshot. They finally tired of the bombardment and deserted the thickets for the open range.

The year 1911 came. Again the river flowed, making seven consecutive flood years. The drift fence in the canyon washed out. In May, Dix received word that cattle were reappearing at Cady. A hasty inspection showed that eighty head of cattle had been grazing above the canyon, and with the advent of warm weather and stock flies, the critters were heading for the sheltering thickets they yet remembered. Lou, the cowpuncher, had been neglecting the cattle and never missed them. They were all driven back and the fence rebuilt.

23 SOME STRANGE ROMANCES AND A SUICIDE ♦ A GERMAN SAILOR LEARNS HIS LESSON ♦ THE FOLLY OF SETTLERS ♦ THE PUSTULE WITH THE FUNKS

"I am going to get a woman. To Hell with this batching. I am tired of it," announced James Mulcahy.

"Where are you going to get one?" inquired a listener.

"I am going to send off for one," replied Jimmy.

He did. Through a matrimonial agency he secured a simple, credulous woman who believed everything Jimmy told her. Everything went well for two or three years until she developed symptoms of insanity. After confinement for a while at the County Hospital, she was returned to her old home in the East, and Jimmy secured a divorce.

Tom Mellon, the old section boss at Yermo, emulated Jimmy and got himself a widow woman with two small children. Occasionally he showed up at a ballgame with the kids and appeared to be fond of them. Their mother was reputed to be a tartar who denied Tom connubial bliss. One day Mellon secured his monthly wages and walked off toward Daggett. He was seen no more. The wife came to the ranch and told her troubles to the Judge, but he could do nothing.

Mrs. Funk had a plump, sixteen-year-old neighbor girl assisting her in the culinary department. Lou came up from Soda Lake to spend a brief holiday. For a year he had been subsisting on beans and canned grub. Three days of Mrs. Funk's appetizing grub convinced Lou that he was in love, and he proposed marriage to the girl. She refused, and he departed wearing a gloomy snoot. She was a nice kid. Twenty-five years later, after two unsuccessful marriages, she grieved her friends by committing suicide.

Now and then, some well-meaning person endeavored to interest Dix in matrimony by delivering a panegyric about some bit of femininity they desired to acquaint him with. They always caused him intense irritation by conveying in what they deemed a subtle and tactful manner the information that she was not too well bred or educated for a galoot living in the desert.

In the fall there came a fresh invasion of settlers who spread over the valley east of the ranch and south of the river. Bill Frakes derisively termed them Sand Lappers. Some took 160-acre homesteads, upon which, to obtain title to the land from the government, they must establish a home for five years. Others filed on Desert Land claims of 320 acres. In order to gain their titles, for four years they had to perform labor on their land worth a specified dollar amount and make certain improvements on their acreage. Most of the homesteaders had some money, and some worked for the owners of the desert land claims. Some of the latter were either wealthy or engaged in business or professions elsewhere. Some were mere speculators intrigued with the belief they were securing cheap land that would soon enhance in value.

One homesteader was a young woman who came for her health and built a substantial adobe house. Her mother and two young women friends lived with her, and the neighbors promptly dubbed the place the Squaw Ranch. One of the young ladies desired to be the local postmistress at Newberry Station. She came to the Judge to secure a legal document.

"I can't certify that you are a spinster," he told her. "I don't know you. You will have to prove that."

"How can I possibly prove such a thing?" she wailed.

They stayed fourteen months and secured title by paying $200 in lieu of further residence and then abandoned the place. The house eventually became a ruin.

A German sailor filed a homestead in the riverbottom and one day set his dog on Frakes's sheep. When they returned home with bloody ears, their owner followed their back trail and saw what happened. He marched the culprit to the scene and, pointing to the tracks, told him what he had done and of the terrible things that would happen to him if he again offended.

The next day, Frakes inadvertently rode by where he was working, and the sailor rushed for a shotgun leaning against a tree. Frakes quickly slid off the opposite side of his horse and leveled his revolver, yelling for him to stop. He did.

"Why did you try to get that gun?" roared Frakes.

"I thought that you wus going to git me," whined the frightened German.

"You damned fool. Ain't you got sense enough to know I could if I wanted to?" replied Frakes. "If you ever pull a fool stunt like that again, I will kill you."

"I don't want to have to kill that damned Dutchman," complained Frakes to Dix. "I don't want trouble with nobody. All I want is to be left alone."

Frakes did not realize that he was a survivor of a vanishing era.

Autos were increasing in the towns, but travel far from habitations was yet regarded as a hazardous venture and rarely undertaken. Model T Fords were the best car. Light in weight, they did not sink deep in the sand, and when they did the passengers could usually shove them out.

The new settlers expended a great deal of labor and money in various ways: drilling wells, building houses, clearing and grading land, and planting orchards. Once in a while, a seeker after knowledge visited the ranch, but about all they cared to know was how many tons of hay was procured from an acre and the price it sold for. Trivial matters, like the law of gravitation and its effect on pumping costs, did not trouble them. They furnished a market for hay, and it was not wise to offend them with dismal forecasts. Unfavorable advice would have been disbelieved. And, of course, the old resident is not supposed to know anything.

One optimistic soul invested $2,200 in a great barn that was used only to store a variegated assortment of implements shipped from an Iowa farm. In after years a new crop of settlers removed the barn piecemeal, together with the house.

"I am partial to alkali," commented another settler who was plowing some land that was almost white with it.

"What this country needs is some good California farmers," declaimed the County Horticulture Commissioner.

"We've had 'em. We've had plenty of them, but they don't stop. They keep right on going," sourly remarked the Judge.

"That ditch of yours looks good to me," observed a keen-looking investigator.

"These newcomers think they can pump it cheaper from wells than we get it from the river," replied the Judge.

"Not me. I have paid for too much distillate in my time," was the rejoinder.

The settlers had one trait in common. Each was determined to make the land conform to his ideas of what it should do.

"I am going to send my soil to the State University and have them analyze it and tell me what to grow," announced a wise one.

Adverse comment from a listener brought only glowering contempt for his ignorance.

The year 1912 brought discord and trouble on the ranch. The Judge discovered that Mr. Funk had appropriated $2,200 of the revenues. Funk and Dix had agreed to forgo wages and to share equally in any money that might become available. Dix had received no wages for three years. Some acrimonious disputes resulted.

Kerckhoff went to Europe for a year's rest and left his affairs in the hands of his secretary, his attorney, and a nephew who was also an attorney. They proposed forming a corporation to manage the property and develop it. Mr. Funk joined them with alacrity. The Van Dykes refused. They offered to sell but declined to exchange their property for stock in a company where they would be minority holders and powerless.

Through connivance the creditors were induced to assign their claims to a Los Angeles bank. Suit was brought and writs of attachment levied. A keeper was placed in charge of the ranch at $3 per day salary. Another was placed in charge of the cattle at Soda Lake at $6 per day.

At various times Clifford had freely bestowed his services in seeking and gathering cattle. The horse he favored was at Soda Lake. Here was an opportunity to repay him. Dix gave him a bill of sale for the horse and saddle and a railway ticket.

"Get there ahead of the deputy and take possession of the horse and saddle before he arrives. Don't surrender it. It can't be taken from you," he admonished Clifford. He followed instructions and retained the horse for many years.

"I will show those galoots I know something about law," growled the Judge. "If I don't, this County has a fine poorhouse I can always go to.

"Don't waste any more money buying grub," he admonished his son. "Kill a cow and make jerky out of it and buy a sack of beans. We will lick that gang yet."

The new alfalfa fields were on the Judge's homestead. During the previous year, Mr. Funk had stacked $1,000 worth of hay there. This property, together with the haystack, was exempt from attachment. Some of the livestock and implements were also exempt. The Van Dykes calmly appropriated them and the hay and proceeded to farm their own lands.

"I will secure an injunction and stop you from using irrigating water," threatened Kerckhoff's secretary.

"You do it just as quick as you can," snorted the Judge. "I will make you pay a fine big bill of damages."

Dix had to make final proof on his desert land claim at the Los Angeles Land Office. The enemy had spread poison there. The Judge was led into a room where an inquisitor plied him with questions and a stenographer rapidly typed the responses.

"Mr. Van Dyke, what is your business?" queried the official.

"I am a farmer," replied the Judge.

"Have you not had any other business?"

"Yes. I am an author," said the Judge.

"Well, we have been informed that you are a lawyer and a good one."

"I can't claim that. I have not practiced law for twenty-five years."

Both the Judge and Dix submitted to a lengthy and rapid examination. At the end, they were asked to sign their statements. They did. No flaws could be found in them. An inspector was sent to view the land. He reported that he could find no fault. The proof was accepted and the patent issued. The enemy made vociferous threats of perjury prosecutions, but nothing came of it.

24 VIOLENCE BREAKS OUT AT THE RANCH ♦ DIX'S TRICKS ♦ AN IMPUDENT WOBBLY AND A SLY WIDOW ♦ DIX VISITS CATALINA ISLAND ♦ All parties continued to dwell upon the attached property. Funk continued to irrigate and harvest the hay under the Sheriff's authority. Old Bob Wilson was the keeper. He disliked the Judge and his son but had to remain neutral. They knew what liberties they could take and managed to cause much irritation to the enemy. Mr. Funk made frequent trips to Los Angeles to consult the attorneys. His retainers challenged Dix to fight. He declined.

"I am not fool enough to fight with hired men," he said.

The Judge was serene about everything and laughed and joked about the situation. The belief that any city sharpers could outwit him in legal matters amused him. But when he learned that a Funk employee had waylaid his son with a club and his son had accepted the challenge and tried to brain his adversary with an iron tool, he became furious. Marching over to the Funk dwelling, he profanely informed all hands that if there was any more fighting on the ranch, he would carry a gun and kill the first man that started it. They believed him, and thereafter peace prevailed.

Time rolled on, and the Sheriff's expense bill rolled up. The Van Dykes were harvesting their hay and selling it.

"Just keep on running up that expense bill. Scuttle the ship and sink it. We don't care," they jeered.

They kept on until after three months the enemy became scared. They had tried to intimidate the Van Dykes and had found the old Judge too keen a lawyer and that in every way the law favored his position.

A compromise was agreed upon, and the Sheriff sold the cattle. They were sacrificed for $5,000. The Sheriff retained $1,700 for his costs. A remnant of the cattle and some range horses went ungathered. Later they were sold for a trivial sum to an enemy of Dix. He demanded a share of the booty for securing the Judge's consent to the sale. It was reluctantly given him, and he now owned a small herd of cattle and horses. He had sold one of the exempted horses for $150 and defiantly retained the money and had extorted a heavy bribe from the buyer of the large herd.

"This is a game of grab stakes. Honor has no place here," he declared.

It all distressed his foes when they learned of his tricks, but he had done nothing illegal.

Kerckhoff returned from Europe and refused to participate in the hostilities. His underlings withdrew. Kerckhoff was an honorable man who disdained trickery and was always fair in his dealings.

Mr. Dieterle deemed himself a promoter. He yet retained a lien for the purchase price of his interest. Now he secured options upon the others. Kerckhoff agreed to sell for cash, Funk for a share of the water. He had a desert land claim upon which he could use it. The Van Dykes agreed to take water for their share in the irrigation system. Of the original ranch they wanted their house and ten acres of land about it. Pleasant fruit trees surrounded it, and they did not want to start another home in the desert. They had plenty of land in addition.

Mr. Funk squawled with misery when he learned they were getting more than he.

"It's the principle of the thing. They should not get more than me," he wailed.

Dieterle secured the contracts and now needed a financial angel. He must build an aqueduct in lieu of the dirt canal and construct a new water tunnel beneath the river. Buel Funk joined him. He was tired of the city, had dissipated most of his wife's fortune, and her health was failing. They wished to be back on the desert. They now had two boys.

The Judge now squawled. He did not want any Funks involved in the irrigation system nor wanted anything to do with any of them. His son overruled his objections. He wanted water to farm with. He did not care who paid for it.

Dieterle had four years in which to complete the work but must furnish definite amounts of water in increasing amounts each year. The year ended with all parties feeling cheerful and looking forward with optimistic hopes. The ending of hostilities caused merriment among the townsmen.

"I knew the Judge would beat that gang. He is too smart for them," observed Bob Greer, who was now living on a little farm in the riverbottom near the canal.

A new year, 1913, came along. The river flowed in a small stream sufficient to maintain the water levels during the summer.

Bill Frakes again had his tranquility disturbed. One evening a young tramp appeared at his home and solicited food. Frakes gave him supper, a bed, and breakfast, and he departed. Frakes now had so many sheep that in winter and spring he kept a herder. The tramp had heard them planning to be away all day. He watched until they left, then he returned and robbed the house. He changed shoes and meandered up the river, concealing his tracks by walking on brush and wading the stream.

Frakes changed his plans and returned before noon. The different shoes disconcerted him until he tracked the tramp to where he had tarried and watched the house. Then Frakes trailed the man down the river and onto the open desert toward the railway station at Newberry. He borrowed a saddlehorse from a settler.

"When I git that damned thief, the only thing going to be needed is a Coroner's jury," he raged.

At Newberry he encountered Fred Johnson, the Constable, who deprived him of his rifle.

"I know where he is. If I kill him I can get out of it easier than you can," he informed the irate sheepman.

The tramp had Frakes's large revolver, but Johnson got the drop on him and he surrendered.

The culprit was impudent and defiant. He was only nineteen years old, and the County Judge was reluctant to sentence him to prison.

"Young man, what did you intend to do with that revolver you had when you were arrested?" he queried.

"I intended to kill anybody who tried to arrest me. That officer got the drop on me with his rifle, so I surrendered."

"I had better have a lunacy commission examine you," commented the Judge.

"I know what I am about. I belong to the Industrial Workers of the World. If anyone has anything and I want it, I have a right to take it. If anyone tries to arrest me and I can kill him, I will do it," he defiantly retorted.

"I can't do my duty and turn you loose. I sentence you to four years in the penitentiary," decreed the Judge.

One year later, the young man and two other prisoners were killed by the prison guards. He had been incorrigible.

Buel began work upon a new flume beneath the river channel. He scooped a ditch down to the water level with team and scraper. Then with mauls his crew drove redwood planks two inches thick and six inches wide in two parallel rows four feet apart. The sand between was pumped out with a centrifugal pump that would pass small stones. The large stones were shoveled out. As the sand was removed, the planks were gradually pounded down. It was the cheapest method that could then be used.

For a cook Buel engaged a middle-aged widow with two children who was traveling with a mule team and wagon. She traded in the outfit for an abandoned homestead with a house that was nearby. From a distant lover she secured funds to purchase chickens. The poor fish thought he was financing a romance. He was, but not for himself. A young laborer enamored with her cooking believed himself in love. He proposed and was accepted. They were married in Barstow. The bride transported herself on a burro, and the groom walked. The chickens furnished the wedding feast. The romance lasted two years. A baby resulted, and the fond father decamped. Ten years later the lady called at the ranch. She was driving a good car and said she had a new husband who was a provider.

A foolish old man selected a farm site in an uninhabited locality fifteen miles south of Daggett and engaged two men to dig a well. He drove a team to Daggett, bought supplies, and departed. Three days later one of his horses was found near town with the harness on and dragging the neck yoke. The next day the well-drillers walked into a town fifty miles up the river and reported the old man had not returned. A telegram to Daggett started a search party. The wagon with a dead horse yet fastened to it was found far from the road. A party of mounted men made a futile search. Four years later, his scattered bones were found two miles from Daggett. He had evidently died of thirst. Coyotes had dragged the remains about, but a watch and a purse revealed his identity.

The Van Dykes rented their alfalfa fields to a homesteader with some big boys. They were competent and took good care of the fields and crops. There was no longer any work in caring for the canal, and for the first time the two Van Dykes had ease and leisure.

Dix spent some time in riding about the Camp Cady range looking after the cattle and horses he was interested in. This had ever been a pleasant relaxation from the ranch. It was not always easy, but it was a change of work. One disagreeable task was crossing the river when flood water was flowing in it. This could not be done except when the river was low, and then it was often unsafe. Horses unused to quicksand become panic-stricken when they find themselves sinking, and they commence plunging and lunging until they become mired.

One had to select a place where it seemed possible to cross, then strip off clothes and wade to the opposite shore, perhaps sinking waist-deep in the icy water. If the crossing was deemed feasible, stakes were set to enable one to walk back and forth in a straight line until the quicksand was packed firm. Then the horse was led over by the bridle lines so as to keep him in the track. If the horse began lunging, one could pull on the lines. If he lay down, the rider must continue to pull on the lines while lashing the horse about the head and nose with a rawhide quirt. This punishment usually would cause the horse to struggle to its feet. It was a situation that tried one's patience to the utmost, and few would attempt it because there was always danger of losing the horse. Wading in quicksand was not a task for timorous souls. However, Dix made such crossings many times without any mishaps.

Dix visited Catalina Island, a famed resort off the Coast. Three days of mingling in crowds of strangers finished him. He did not know how to mix with them. He could have been happy camping out alone, but the crowds made him lonely. He returned and with a team journeyed to the San Bernardino Mountains. The sixty-mile journey took him three days. He camped beneath great pines beside a mountain lake filled with large trout and wandered about the mountains with a saddle and a pack horse. The mountain people were a friendly folk and regarded him as one of their own kind. The air was cool and bracing, and the soughing of the pines was sweet music.

Here, Dix had plenty of time for meditating, and he decided that he had been a fool. He had spent twelve successive summers toiling in the desert. When he made the contract with Dieterle, Dix had canceled a claim for nine years' wages. When he thought of the many years of arduous labor and how little recreation or spending of money he had enjoyed, he resolved to live differently in the future, and he kept his resolve. He continued to do plenty of work, but he no longer made a religion of it.

25 THE JUDGE TAKES IT EASY ◆ WHISKEY USED IN MILLING ◆ JOHN MUIR'S FINAL CALL ◆ WORLD WAR I ◆ OLD-TIMERS BEWILDERED: THE BUCKET OF BLOOD SALOON SELLS ICE CREAM ◆ AN ACRIMONIOUS CAMPAIGN ◆ MORE OF DIX'S TRICKS ◆ The Judge enjoyed his summers on the desert. No one ever heard him complain of the heat. He liked it. In the cool part of the day he would putter about in his vegetable garden and spend his leisure on the veranda poring over his beloved tomes in Greek and Latin.

Many years before, he had wandered about hunting deer among the hills and mountains of San Diego County. There he envisioned the possibility of damming a river where it flowed between two mountains and conveying the water to coastal lands. He told his friend Henry Keller of it:

"If you can ever get your hands on $200,000 and the time is ripe, I will show it to you," he told him.

The time was now deemed ripe, and he spent time with Keller touring in an auto over the rugged country he had once traversed on foot and with horses. For this, the Judge received $1,300 in engineering fees. This came in very handy. The dam and irrigation system was built, but the Judge had no connection with the promoting of it. He did derive much satisfaction from the completion of a project he had long dreamed of.

The new settlers were increasing in number and displaying much enthusiasm. One planted a grain crop. The winter rains were sufficient to allow it to grow a few inches high. The range horses nibbled the fresh shoots off, and the planter wailed dismally over the valuable crop the horses had destroyed. He built an expensive fence around his field, but he departed before another winter came.

The winter of 1914 was warm and wet. Rain drenched California, and grass and crops grew luxuriantly over the state. January brought a large flood down the river. Most of it poured through the river ditch that Dix had dug and widened it into a large channel. From then on, the great canal was never endangered because the flood waters passed down the opposite side of the riverbed.

In April came an election for school trustee. The section boss's wife was the candidate. The old fossils in the village had been the only voters at such elections, and usually they were a mere formality. This time, however, the candidate was disliked, and some of the young fellows persuaded Buel Funk to run in opposition to her. He announced his candidacy on election day, and the boys raced around town persuading reluctant voters to go to the polls. She lost to Buel.

"They did that just for damned meanness," her husband proclaimed.

Buel was a family man, and the old fossils could not squawk, but they did plenty of squawking after future elections.

Hay was cheap elsewhere in the state, but the ranchers received a good price because the new settlers were not yet producing any for sale.

After the river ceased flowing, Buel resumed work in water development. He also financed a mining project. Some local miners milled silver ore from Calico in a small plant. It did not pay, and some opined that too much whiskey was used in the milling. Buel had built a six-room house on the ranch for his family.

Dix's renters had quit, and he had to operate the ranch himself. But when hot weather came, he left the place in charge of a foreman and went back to the mountains. The Judge declined an invitation to go. He had been in those mountains forty years before when the journey was arduous. They had no charms for him now:

"I don't want to go. They are all spoiled. Every place you go the damned tenderfeet have been."

Years later his son learned to feel the same way about the mountains. He spent the summer there and leased a cabin site from the government. This was in a little ravine with a spring surrounded by steep hills. Dix thought that tenderfeet never would build cabins on the hills, but in time they did.

John Muir came to the ranch for a visit, the first in four years. Before this he had been strong and healthy and talked glowingly of the travels he was contemplating. He journeyed to South Africa. Far in the interior he stopped at a hotel maintained by a Scotchman who had purchased every one of Muir's books. He was so overjoyed at meeting Muir that he declined any remuneration from him.

He went to South America to investigate the report that conifers grew there. On the ship he fraternized with a crew of American woodsmen going to cut raw lumber. He evaded a grand reception planned for him at the city where they disembarked. Instead, he went with the lumbermen up the Rio de la Plata. At the lumber camp the superintendent came down to the boat landing to inspect the crew. It had cost much money to bring the men, and when he saw Muir he ejaculated:

"What in Hell did you bring that old galoot for?"

When Muir turned to look at him he cried, "My God, it's Scotty!"

Many years before they had been cronies in the redwoods of California. Muir had never recovered from the hardships he endured then.

The first day he arrived at the ranch, he called on the Judge. He looked feeble and ill. The next day his daughter found him in a stupor. A wire to Los Angeles summoned a doctor and nurse. When they arrived, they placed him on a train and took him to a hospital in Los Angeles. He died a few hours later. He was seventy-six years old and could not survive the attack of double pneumonia.*

Muir's wife had been the only surviving child of a thrifty pioneer from whom she had inherited much property. Under Muir's management it had increased. On her death, she divided it among Muir and their two daughters. Muir never speculated. All he knew to do with money was to poke it into a bank. He knew no way to get fun out of it. His idea of a wild time was to go off into the solitudes and live like a wild animal. Even when he traveled, he usually received free transportation and often had his expenses eagerly paid by admirers. No one had any idea of the extent of his wealth until various banks sent statements of his accounts. Then it was revealed that he had $100,000 in cash, in addition to as much property.

---

*Dix's account of Muir's taking sick at Daggett accords generally with Wolfe's (347–48).

Buel had expended most of his wife's inheritance from her mother and had been short of funds. He had toiled with his workmen and economized in various ways. Now he blossomed out and acquired a fancy saddlehorse and a racing automobile and tried to be a sport.

In August the First World War began, and in time its dire effects upon business became evident. With the advent of cool weather came numerous destitute men thrown out of employment in other states. They were glad to work for their board and trivial wages—anything to get through the winter. Dix gathered a crew and began grading land. He continued through the winter and prepared a large acreage. The Judge growled about the growing debts, but the water supply was increasing, and Dix borrowed from Buel at 9 percent interest secured by a mortgage on the Judge's land.

The ranch was again leased to a tenant who was adept at securing cheap labor and did much grading in return for cattle and horses. Dix gathered his range cattle and horses and quit the stock business. He decided that there was no longer any profit to be made that way.

The County Supervisors issued saloon licenses yearly in July. Most of the County was dry under various local option laws. The prohibitionists were numerous and strong in the San Bernardino Valley. The drys succeeded in annexation of a citrus-growing district where most of the voters were dry and then called for a local option election. It failed. Then they stormed the Supervisors' meeting and vociferously objected to the granting of saloon licenses. The desert was the sole remaining part of the County where saloons were yet allowed. Awed by the political pressure from their dry districts, a majority of the Board of Supervisors decreed that no more saloons should be licensed.

Alex Falconer was the only surviving saloonist in Daggett, and he began dispensing soft drinks and ice cream. Little liquor had been sold recently. No mines were operating, and the old patrons who had often come to "blow a stake" had disappeared or died. San Bernardino, the County Seat, also voted dry at the election. That had long been a town where vice flourished and many came to blow in. Times were changing, but the old-timers were bewildered. They could not accept that the era in which they had lived was passing.

It was another election year for the Judge and the Constable. The Judge never heeded such affairs. If his constituents desired his services, that was their concern, not his. They had to take the required measures to ensure his candidacy appearing on the ballot and race about electioneering for him. They always did.

Fred Johnson was a candidate for reelection as Constable. He was opposed by Bob Wilson, now seventy years of age and nearly blind. He was living on a meager Civil War pension and desired the salary of twenty dollars a month and the prestige of office.

Fred Johnson's son had been accidently shot and killed while scuffling with a man for the possession of a revolver, and Fred removed his family to San Bernardino. He now had a job supervising other railway officers stationed at various points on the desert. However, he resided part of the time in Daggett, where another railway officer was stationed and was his deputy.

There was now a new element in Daggett. It gathered in the schoolhouse on Sundays and made loud, self-righteous noises. These people opposed Johnson because he made no effort to gather evidence against Alex, who was accused of surreptitiously selling liquor. It was not the duty of a Constable to do detective work, but his opponents cared nothing for that. It was an acrimonious campaign. Bob expected the support of the remaining old-timers, who had long known him. They knew him too well and voted for Johnson, who was reelected. Old Bob was so chagrined and disappointed that he moved to San Bernardino. A few years later he suddenly dropped dead in a restaurant.

Dix had not rounded up the wild range horses at Camp Cady in many a year. The horses knew all the fences in the riverbottom and evaded the gates. On the sandy floor of the valley they could easily outrun a saddlehorse encumbered with a rider. Occasionally one could be caught, but all efforts to corral the band failed. Dix and two others claimed ownership, but there were many unbranded horses among them, and no one could prove ownership. Dix learned that the other two were preparing for a private roundup. He had not been invited.

Dix arranged a surprise. The horses roamed over the open desert fifteen miles from the ranch and as far as the other side of the Calico Hills and went to the river for water.

26 CHASING WILD HORSES, CONT. ♦ CARS COME TO DAGGETT ♦ MARRIAGE MARKET DECIDED BY ELECTION ♦ DELUSIONS OF GRANDEUR ♦ A TEACHER ELOPES — THE BOYS CHEER! ♦ BARNEY OLDFIELD SPEEDS THROUGH DAGGETT ♦ A TOUGH RANCH WOMAN FOLLOWS HER HUSBAND'S VISION ♦ With one helper, Dix rode out onto the range at night and slept on the ground. At daylight they were on the hunt. Their well-fed horses could run fast for a few miles, driving the quarry up into the rock slopes of the Calicos, where the sharp rocks quickly bruised their unshod hooves. These steep hills formed a barrier on one side, with the riders on the other. By the time the horses passed around the end of the hills, they were footsore and in strange territory. In this state, they thought no more of dodging around the riders but only of running from them. On the east side of the ranch and one mile from the house, Dix had torn a large gap in the fence. He also left a saddled horse waiting in a nearby corral. There Dix could quickly mount the fresh horse and easily chase the wild ones through the gap in the fence. In a few days, the horses were all gathered. Those with brands were released.

The other claimants squawked, denouncing the procedure as larceny. One of them personally upbraided Dix, who just laughed and extended a cordial invitation to come to the ranch and pick out any horses that belonged to him. The man never came, because he knew he could neither identify his horses nor prove his ownership.

One night Dix and his helper camped at an abandoned homestead beside a well dug sixty feet deep. Tying their riatas together, they drew up some foul water giving evidence that there were plenty of dead rodents at the bottom. It was far too obnoxious to drink, and Dix proceeded to boil coffee in it. While doing this, he observed his companion, who was a newcomer, washing his face.

"You've got me beat if you can wash your face in that stinking stuff," he said. "I have got to have a drink, but I can't wash my face in that water."

An organized effort had been made to promote a transcontinental highway along the route of the Santa Fe Railway. It was named the National Old Trails Highway. When a railroad is built, a wagon road usually parallels it. This wagon road was marked with signs, and a few automobile adventurers made the trip from coast to coast, but until 1915 there was little travel. This year several hundred cars came from the East, and one loud-mouthed young squirt made the ridiculous prophecy that someday passengers would be hauled across the desert in automobiles in competition with the railways.

Travel was a hazardous venture. The roads were ruts in the soil with plenty of chuckholes filled with dust. In many localities, ten miles an hour was the limit for safe driving during daylight. Travel ceased at night. Everyone carried camping equipment and was prepared to camp anywhere beside the road. Auto camps had not yet been dreamed of, and the early ones furnished no bedding or dishes. Tires were expensive and poorly made. All garages specialized in repairing them and in welding broken springs or supplying new ones. There were no gas pumps. The fuel was carried to the auto in a bucket.

Yet automobiles ruined the market for light horses. In courting girls, the rural yokel with a black-topped buggy and driving horse had always had the advantage over the town boy, who had to hire a livery plug. Now it was the other way around, and the townsman with a car could have his pick of the girls. Tractors were coming into use, and special schools taught the art of driving and caring for them. Still, large horses remained in demand, and few people believed that they would be replaced by trucks, most of which had solid-rubber tires and frequently needed repairs.

Another school election rolled around. The boys had prepared for it. Mr. McMillan, the incumbent, was up for election as trustee. The boys disapproved of Mc. His wife had been a teacher, but he was averse to hiring young ones. He liked them old and homely. Tom McCue, an exemplary young man twenty-five years old, was selected for his opponent. There were now a few cars in Daggett, but few of the miners and ranchers had any. They were very much gratified when one of the boys called and offered them a trip to town and return, all free of cost, with a good cigar to smoke. They were glad to vote for a popular young man. The boys insisted that it was their aim to boost the marriage market by getting attractive young teachers.

Tom was elected. McMillan and his supporters were mad. They loudly denounced the rebels and their methods, but they only provoked laughter and raillery.

Dix leased the ranch to the foreman, who had been employed the previous year. He got delusions of grandeur. He bought a new buggy, a typewriter, and an office desk. He averaged three trips a day to town and wasted much time dispensing wisdom to any loafers who would listen to him. There were many men seeking employment, and he was adept at inducing some to work three or four months for a saddle-horse and their board, clothes, and tobacco. He kept plenty of help.

Buel's crew continued developing water on the river, and the supply at the ranch was increasing. He now had plenty of money. His wife had long before given him an absolute power of attorney to do anything he desired with her money and property. She never questioned his acts. His father continued to work like a hired hand, and his mother cooked for the help.

Dix again spent the summer in the mountains and built a small cabin on the lot he had leased. He left one man grading land on the ranch. This was a big young Lithuanian who seemed never to tire. He had learned how to grade the land when it was marked out for him. He lived in the little shack on the homestead and believed the $55 a month he received to be big wages. He spent nothing except for food. In the old country he had eaten only two meals a day.

"I try that again, but I can't do it no more," he said.

The trustees hired a young teacher. She was not single long. She became infatuated with Roy Kemper, a young telegraph operator, and eloped with him. Her parents had approved of another suitor whom they well knew. He afterwards married her sister. The teacher's marriage to Kemper cheered the boys. Twenty-six years later, the Kempers came with their two daughters to an Old-Timers Picnic held on the ranch.

This year there was a road race across the desert from Los Angeles to Phoenix, Arizona. It was nearly 500 miles and was called an endurance run. It surely was, both for the cars and the passengers. Such races were paid for by auto manufacturers and were deemed valuable advertising, especially when only two sets of tires were needed. Barney Oldfield, the famous racer, was a participant. The Daggett population all turned out to see Barney pass. Auto racers were famous men with great renown.

The trustees now hired a handsome young Norwegian girl for the new teacher. She became very popular, and there was speculation about who the winner would be.

Bill Frakes quit Camp Cady in disgust. Neighbors were getting too plentiful, and some grumbled about the depredations of his sheep. He now had 800. He took them to Soda Lake, but for some reason many died there, and he moved to a desert area in Arizona. He lived until past eighty years but was almost totally blind in his last years.

George Willis had gradually accumulated a small herd of cattle and horses and now moved to Ord Mountain. Beside a great heap of granite boulders at the elevation of 4,000 feet, he established a home in which he and his wife were to dwell for ten years. Indian pictographs on the rocks led him to believe there had once been a spring there. He dug and found water at twenty feet. He built a rough shack with a dirt floor and a piece of canvas hung over it for a door. The shack was never improved. His wife hoisted water for the cattle with a rope and bucket, standing straddle on two planks and drawing it up between her knees. In winter she gathered rocks and built stone walls that eventually totaled many hundreds of tons. She was clearing land for the gardens and orchard that George would depict to her in rosy hues. George had the gift of the gab and could draw entrancing word pictures.

At Camp Cady there once was a military reservation that included 1,600 acres of bottomland. It was just worth fencing for a stock pasture if one could get it for nothing, but the government sold it at public auction in small parcels of forty acres or less. When the parcel upon which Frakes's house stood was sold, the buyers good-naturedly declined to bid against him. In later years the various tracts were bought and gathered in one ownership.

27 THE UPLIFTING OF DAGGETT ♦ THE HEN CLUB GLARES AT THE HARMONY GANG OVER CHICKEN BONES ♦ DIX GETS IN HIS LICKS ♦ DAGGETT DOOMED TO ITS PAST ♦ As to Daggett, forty years ago it was a moribund little village that had dwindled to one store, one restaurant, and one saloon. The producing mines that once supported it had ceased operations, and the new railways intercepted trade that had formerly benefited the town.

Life was dull, and little of interest occurred. Some of the women never left the village and seldom ventured more than a short distance from their houses. Local travel, even with the best of horses and light rigs, was tiring. The roads were mere ruts in the loose soil. Autos had a narrower gauge than wagons, and either ruined the track for the other to follow.

Auto travel was a nuisance. The machines were tricky, unreliable critters, and their tires poorly made and easily disabled. Anyway, there was no place to go. The nearest villages were no more interesting than Daggett, and a round trip to even the closest ones required most of a day. The boredom of civilized life in Daggett made a fertile breeding ground for squabbles.

Daggett had never been a pious town, but now it became dominated by a sanctimonious clique who gathered in the schoolhouse each Sunday and indulged in noisy manifestations of piety. Fragments of various sects composed it and were welded together by a mutual antipathy for Catholics.

During the week they gained satisfaction by criticizing the nonconformists in the village and saying mean things about Alex Falconer and his saloon. He did not have much patronage, but it gave them something to squawk about.

Because of the reformers, schoolteachers were marooned in unhappy surroundings. There was a two-week Christmas vacation when they might escape temporarily, but they only received $75 a month and had to hoard money for summer vacations. The trustees quizzed applicants about their religious affiliations and beliefs. Only those were selected who were past the bloom of youth and could be expected to be inured to a drab life and find consolation in teaching Sunday school and manifesting piety. They were ever subject to censorious eyes watching for any indication of frivolity. Under those conditions, teachers seldom lasted more than one term.

One of the reform gang was a middle-aged spinster, a minister's daughter's daughter, who came for a prolonged visit with relatives who were among the elect. She was a gentle, well-bred, and pious lady bursting with altruism and an urge to perform good deeds for the welfare of humanity.

She decided that Daggett needed an uplifting influence and that it was her mission to bring it about.

She did it, all right.

She organized a women's club. The proceedings were so secret that nothing about its activities were divulged, and even its name was not revealed. The irreverent male scoffers of the village derided it and dubbed it "The Hen Club." It lasted only a month, then blew up with a bang, like a dynamite explosion. Evil gossiping by some of the members about others was rumored to have incited the uproar, but no man could understand what it was about. It was impossible for three women to get together without two of them making snoots at the other.

One faction secured an empty store building, installed an old piano, and indulged in dances and social gatherings. They called themselves the Harmony Club, but the malcontents dubbed them the Jarmony Gang. Occasionally, a member of one faction would contribute some news to the local paper published in Barstow and include some sarcastic item about their enemies. The offended ones vented their wrath on the harassed editor:

"What can I do?" he wailed. "They bring in news items that appear all right to me. I don't know anything about their scraps."

At the time, plenty of water flowed in the Mojave River, and numerous old trees grew between Daggett and Barstow. Especially beautiful was a grove of large, spreading cottonwoods in the riverbottom two miles west of Daggett. It was a delightful picnic ground, where for many years a town picnic was held at the end of the school year in the late spring.

The cottonwoods gave plenty of deep shade, and the water flowing in the irrigation canal along the river's border furnished a fine playground for the children to wade and paddle. Various conveyances drawn by horses and mules transported all comers.

People flocked to the picnics because the women vied in supplying good eats of home-cooked food. No other feasts like them could be found in these rural parts. Everyone enjoyed a pleasant day and went home well pleased with the day's events. Liquor was never taken to these picnics.

Mrs. Shook was a newcomer who purchased the cottonwood grove and erected a house beside the canal. She was a kind and gentle old lady eager to make friends. The discord in Daggett distressed her. It was difficult for her to remain inactive, and she devised a plan to restore peace and harmony.

She invited both factions to a moonlight picnic in her grove and promised them a feast of fat young chickens. She erected some small tepees beneath a wide-spreading cottonwood and in various ways tried to make the meetingplace resemble what she believed an Indian camp should look like.

The Harmony Club decided to combine a hayride with the feast. Dix and four horses hauled the Harmony Club on a hayrack covered with freshly mown alfalfa. They were the last to arrive.

They found their enemy already ensconced in the tepees. They were incensed and demanded to be taken home. The teamster was a vulgar man without any feminine affiliations and rudely refused their request:

"Nothing doing," he told them.

"You knew what to expect," he continued. "You accepted Mrs. Shook's invitation, and you are under obligations to your hostess to remain and be courteous."

They listened with bad grace. The belligerents spent the entire evening glowering at each other.

This did not affect their appetites, however. They consumed all of the chickens and later expressed their appreciation by scolding Mrs. Shook for inviting their enemies to the feast.

Because of the bitterness, the town picnics that had been held early each summer ended, and it was a long time before memories dimmed and another picnic was held.

EPILOGUE

Daggett Today

WE COME FULL CIRCLE, back to scenes in the Introduction, in a parenthesis of history.

A little less than three miles north of today's Daggett, travelers weary of hours of desert driving turn off the interstate and stream up the two-lane paved road toward Calico, the mining town that once shipped its wealth to booming Daggett. The travelers are in for a treat. Calico is a remarkable place, boasting both dramatic scenery and dramatic history.

As the road gradually rises from the desert floor, the tourists see directly ahead of them a mass of mountains striated with bands of pinks and purples (best seen at sunset). There seems no way into this range, but they slowly enter a broad canyon that after a few minutes turns into the hills and begins closing around them. The walls grow abruptly steeper, then there before them, of all things, clinging wildly to the steep slopes on either side is a town out of the nineteenth century.

The visitors face the pleasure of the impossible. The surrounding hillsides and canyons are laced with thirty miles of shafts and tunnels. From these in the 1880s poured a bonanza, millions of dollars of silver, the largest silver strike in Southern California's history. The town boomed, its main street ringing with the music and commotion of twenty-two saloons. Twice fire ravaged the town, but as long as silver was in the ground, the town bounced back. Then, as inevitably happens, the precious ore ran out, and for decades the buildings slumped into ever deeper ruin.

Now, visitors can get the authentic flavor of the place at its spiciest peak of prosperity from several fine tours. A guide dressed in period clothes, complete with battered hat and old pistol stuck in his belt, strolls with bands of tourists as he discusses the town's history. Past the gingerbread theater, crowded for the show, they hear the audience inside booing the villain in a play from a hundred years ago. Up on a hilltop, at the one-room schoolhouse crowned with a cupola and its desks waiting primly for children, visitors learn that more than greed was important to the community's life a century ago.*

People making a circuit of Calico on the narrow-gauge train marvel at the steep streets below and at the caves dug into the hillsides, the homes where miners of humble means lived. The more adventurous can take a self-guided mine tour, feeling their way through the dimly lit labyrinths — until, climbing a ladder, all at once out they pop into the bright sunlight, blinking and for a moment disoriented. Below, the streets teem with people, banners fly, and the strains of honky-tonk float up on the gusting mountain winds.

Restored by the Knott family in the 1950s and now a county park, the preserved ghost town of Calico, one of the few of its kind, is a splendid example of exciting history informatively presented. Especially exciting from this height, since the surrounding desert, spiked with range on range of mountains off into the mists, seems to have so little to offer.

So gazing in an idle moment, few people would notice the town of Daggett to the south, out there in the far distance. It's no more than a splotch of green beside the bright, sandy band of the dry Mojave River. Of course, as we've seen, Daggett, too, had its uproarious days, but of these, unlike Calico, little is officially preserved. If by some chance a tour bus pulled into Daggett, lurching where the pavement turns to dirt, the passengers in their air-conditioned comfort would likely gawk, knowing that there had been some mistake.

People getting off, stretching their legs as they squint against the sun, might note the impressively broad and sandy railroad right of way. Its multiple tracks and frequent trains split the town lengthwise down the middle. On either side Daggett hunches, its modest houses,

---

*See Lucy Bell Lane's memoir, *Calico Memories*.

most of them fenced against straying cattle, "sprawled out," as Dix says, "on both sides of the railway tracks." If the visitors walk up a graveled street, they might bump into the small Community Center on the north side of town near the volunteer fire department and a surprisingly pleasant little park. But for that, all is quiet. Like many desert creatures, the people seem to have hunkered down in their burrows against the heat.

The amenities? Over there across the Santa Fe's steel ribbons is what looks like a restaurant, but it's much too small to handle a busload of famished tourists. They'd do better to pillage the Desert Market on whose dirt apron the bus behind them shimmers. There they could feast on beef jerky, beer, and Twinkies. If they want a hairdo, the New You Salon across the tracks might be open. Other than that, Daggett is not a place for people itching to spend the money in their pockets.

Such tourists wouldn't know that nearby a borax works once flourished or that miners from Calico often dissipated their dollars in Daggett's noisy saloons. If not all, much of the evidence of those wild days is gone. It would take a sharp-eyed historian armed with esoteric knowledge to recognize the stubs of timbers protruding from the sand over by the river as relics of borax processing. Would he be able to make out the dim line of the old railroad cutting across the lower slopes of Elephant Mountain that once brought wealth to Daggett from the Calico area? And if by an even stranger chance a few of our visitors were to wander out of town and stumble upon Daggett's graveyard among the desert scrub, they'd see, well, old graves, a good number of them unmarked, many of them piled with rocks to discourage dogs and wolves, and crosses tumbled about helter-skelter. Though here and there a modern granite monument testifies to family remembrances, they, too, are dimming as the decades pass and those who remember die. For the most part, it is an eerie, abandoned place.

Back on the bus, they'd decide, quite rightly, that, like some of the other desert towns widely scattered hereabouts, Daggett had its heyday, as the old, peeling, false-front stores, now boarded up, attest. But those days are gone forever.

I'd like to vote for keeping it that way. The Knott family and San Bernardino County have done a praiseworthy job with Calico, and they deserve our thanks and support. What, then, should be done with Daggett? Imagine a well-intentioned millionaire turned enthusiastic local historian doing something similar. Though the Bucket of Blood Saloon is long gone, he could erect a replica, dig out the old Daggett ditch running through town behind the Community Center, and show how the lifeblood of water once flowed across the desert to the Van Dyke Ranch. Then at the ranch itself, now in ruins, with the rubble of fireplaces rising over the sandy flats and cactus clumps growing in old cellar holes, we could have markers numbered to correspond with brochures for self-guided tours.

History, in its broadest terms, is the story of the past, and it is fascinating not only for itself but because it gives us a context, and thereby tells us more richly who we are. And the more we know, the more we'll understand. That, however, creates a problem, one of those irresolvable sticking points of the human condition. All history is valuable. And all towns, no matter how apparently insignificant, are valuable and like to think of themselves as special. If we try to stop time in Daggett at a certain point, why not neighboring Yermo or Newberry? Should we say Daggett because it boasts a place in John Steinbeck's Pulitzer Prize–winning novel, *The Grapes of Wrath*? Right there, across the street from Beryl Bell's house, the one with the oddly curved roof, stood the very agricultural inspection station where Mrs. Joad smuggled the dead grandmother into California.

It's a fascinating tidbit, but no doubt Yermo, Newberry, and Amboy had their murders and scandals, the writhings of human hearts to make many a novel, that could top Daggett's literary claim to fame. According to one ideal, we could totally recreate history, dredging up from the past as with some virtual-reality machine everything, everyone, and all words and acts that ever happened. That would challenge one's sanity, and in any case it is an impossible, endlessly frustrating goal. What was done at Calico is noble, but it is a special circumstance, limited geographically to one or two canyons and dramatically unique as a mining boom town with a short, intense, and colorful history. Such a ghost town lends itself to being sprayed with plastic. A similar approach to Daggett would not work. There, history is too dispersed, too specialized, an ongoing process, and it's not the stuff that when blazoned on billboards inspires tourists to turn off the freeway.

A parallel example might be drawn with genealogy. Many Americans delve into their family histories not because their ancestors led great charges or composed great symphonies but because knowing their past enriches them. And understanding one family, even if we are not directly part of it, helps us to understand broader human workings. In this sense, I think that Daggett particularly deserves attention because it is at once typical and unique in unexpected ways. Its virtues are not the virtues of Calico; they are more challenging because they are more subtle, and in their own special way they reveal rather different aspects than does Calico to the north, or, for that matter, going to the opposite extreme, other desert towns lost in anonymity.

First of all, at something more than a hundred years, Daggett has a relatively long history of white occupation compared to the rest of the Mojave. This is true because Daggett, on the railroad, became the supply base for booming Calico and for other mining districts as far north as Death Valley. It also was on an important east-west roadway for wagon travel that later became the famous Route 66, running smack through the middle of town beside the railroad. In those desert places, Daggett had an essential—water—upwelling nearby in the Mojave River that made borax processing possible and first brought in large-scale agriculture. And the hope for the latter brought in the Van Dykes.

With the Van Dykes came a special element, and we begin a delicate shift from the chemistry of history to its alchemy, into qualities indefinable but nonetheless influential. Educated, well-known, and forceful, Theodore became one of the area's largest landowners as well as its justice of the peace. He created something of a dynasty in the town's brief span, one passed on to his son. For Theodore brought more than himself to Daggett. A learned man with the connections of a powerful family that went back through the nation's history to Colonial days, writer and developer Theodore had strong links to the outside world. They were intellectual as well as financial, and drew to the ranch such lights as John Muir and John Burroughs and Muir's daughter Helen, who stayed to create her own, extended story. And most of all, Dix wrote about Daggett in exceptional ways, leaving what most communities out there don't have, a record of the complex changes taking place in the town.

Furthermore as to alchemy, Daggett has inspired the interest of local historians — or, to put it the other way around, has inspired locals to become historians — as well as attracting some outsiders. Part of the Community Center houses the Daggett Museum, a modest but well-done repository, impressive in light of the town's tiny size. And six miles up the road in the city of Barstow is the Mojave River Valley Museum, a larger organization supporting exploration of the entire region's history.

What's to be done from here on out? Revealing how over the years a frontier town was dragged kicking and screaming into the twentieth century, Daggett's contributions will not be as pyrotechnic as Calico's. Slowly, for example, through John Muir's correspondence we're beginning to understand the profound impact his daughter's stay at the ranch and marriage into a Daggett family had on the famous writer and conservationist. The whole mess at the ranch over water and property rights, typical of much of the West, awaits further investigation. In addition to such things, some areas are almost totally unexplored.

To walk across the Van Dyke Ranch with Dix's nephew, Alan Golden, is to feel history beneath your feet. Here, the former orchards of peaches and nectarines and the hundreds of acres of deep alfalfa, once an agricultural dream in the middle of one of North America's driest places, have returned to sand and prickly pear. Alan, a powerful man in his sixties, son of Dix's sister, Mary, swings a strong arm out, pointing to where the thick, high arch of trees once spanned the old ranch road, making it look like an English country lane. Over there was the Indian Camp, where his mother remembered that Paiutes, clinging to the old, tribal ways, paused in their wanderings. In the opposite direction was the Honey House, named for nearby bee-hives, where Alan lived as a boy. His face glows as the childhood memories pass over him. At night, the family reads in the light of kerosene lamps.

Alan remembers Jimmy, a patient old horse unperturbed by children climbing over him, and his own horse, Smokey. And here, Alan points to a handsome, fieldstone chimney rising out of a mound of bricks, the house where he was born in 1932. The place burned down when Alan was only a few months old—mice gnawing on kitchen matches—and his mother nearly didn't get him out in time as the dry, wooden building whooshed into a cone of flame.

We trudge happily along, stories floating to Alan's mind with every pile of debris. The blacksmith shop where young Alan, mistakenly picking up a piece of hot metal, burned his hands. He still winces.

"What's this, Alan?" I say when we come to a chaos of boards, what must have been another wooden house, looking as if it were flattened and scattered about by a recent whirlwind.

"Why, that's Mamie's place," he tells me, surprised that I would have to ask, since everyone knew Mamie.

"Mamie who?"

And that takes us back to the Daggett graveyard. And to another important story waiting to be told.

There you'll find Alan's father and mother, as well as Dix and other relatives, all with handsome granite headstones, buried in the Golden plot. Strangely, however, on the extreme north edge, crowded in beside Dix is a rather small, unmarked grave with a creosote bush or two growing out of it. For years people wondered who lay in the "mystery" grave.

According to Alan, a reliable source of information, this is "Mamie," a nickname for Mary Beal. She was from Illinois, came out to the ranch early in the twentieth century for her health and, supported by her physician father, stayed until she died decades later.*

*The primary printed sources for Mary Beal are a small but informative booklet by Lucile Weight, *The Floral World of Mary Beal,* and Peter Wild's "Mary Beal: Pioneer Botanist on the Mojave Desert." The personal papers of Harold and Lucile Weight contain much further information.

Obviously, Alan liked this engaging woman, an amateur botanist who roamed the desert studying plants. He points with the pride of memory to the very stump beside the wreckage of her home that this slight woman used for a boost when mounting her horse. Shortly before he died, Uncle Dix married Alan at Mary's house. With more than a hundred guests, Alan winks, the wedding was a "big bash" for such a small town. After Mary Beal died in the 1960s, Alan handled her affairs.

She sounds like a lively and enjoyable person. She certainly lived a narrow life, though her focus on desert plants must have brought her keen satisfaction. Still, who besides those fortunate enough to know her, or by chance distant relatives piecing together the family tree, would be at all interested in an unmarried woman who spent her adult years living on an isolated ranch and wandering the desert? A life for the novelist to ponder, perhaps, but not the historian.

This shows how careful one must be to guard against casual dismissal of anyone or anything. The population of the Mojave Desert in the early days was so small that all people are important in fitting together a puzzle with few pieces. To overlook one might be to leave a big hole in the picture. It turns out that Mary Beal, for instance, was no mere putterer with plants. Though an amateur, she was one of the early pioneers of botany in the Mojave. Cooperating with the University of California at Berkeley, she collected specimens and published many exact articles about the ways of burroweed and lip ferns.*

"Well and good," you might say. That might be of interest to someone studying the history of botany, but that surely is a rare and specialized field.

Yet the contributions of the tiny horsewoman to science may well be only tangentially related to an understanding of much larger subjects going far beyond the Mojave Desert. Mary Beal was active at a time when people were broadening their intellectual and aesthetic curiosity, becoming fascinated about America's deserts beyond their promise of riches. In this sense, she was a bellwether of cultural

---

*See, for example, her "These Plants Sponge Upon Their Neighbors" and "Lip-Ferns on the Desert."

change. And she fits more specifically into the mosaic. Despite com-
puters, it's amazing how serendipity continues to play a vital role in
some research. Browsing through John Muir's correspondence at the
University of the Pacific in Stockton, California, you find Mary Beal
writing Muir on March 3, 1910, from Pasadena. She says she's a friend
of naturalist John Burroughs, who has told her about Helen Muir's
continuing recovery on the desert. Mary is sick, she further writes (of
what illness she doesn't say); would Muir be kind enough to tell her
about the Van Dykes' ranch? Then some months later, on May 14,
1910, Clara Barrus writes John Muir saying how glad she is that Helen
now has such a good companion as Mary Beal.* Barrus, it turns out,
was Burroughs' mistress, and she likely visited the ranch with him.†
And even long after Burroughs' death, Beal is carrying on correspondence with Burroughs' son, Julian.‡

What was going on? How involved and influential was the inter-
play of Mary Beal and others in the national web of relationships with
a nexus at the Van Dyke Ranch? At this point, we simply don't know.
Despite decades of study, new revelations about Muir and Burroughs
keep coming to the surface, and I note that biographies of the two
men are skimpy indeed on their travels through the Mojave and their
visits to the Van Dyke Ranch in Daggett. The tantalizing thing is
rumors about the existence of Mary Beal's journals. They may contain very little of historical import; on the other hand, they may have
a significant bearing on understanding not only their writer and the
region but also two important national figures of the time.

Mary Beal is but one case. There's the strange situation with

---

*The John Muir correspondence is widely available in *The Microform Edition of the
John Muir Papers, 1858–1957.*
†Renehan documents the persistent philandering of the nation's best-known naturalist of that day (137–39).
‡A Daggett resident kindly let me read through three of the letters in his possession
from Julian Burroughs to Mary Beal. They were long and chatty, indicating a lengthy
exchange. It should be added that Mary Beal wrote a tender reminiscence of Burroughs' visit to the ranch in 1911. See her "When John O' Birds Saw Calico." Especially valuable is the dramatic photo of the aged and patriarchal Burroughs standing
with the young Miss Beal before the tent house where she first lived at the ranch (3).

Helen's husband, Buel Funk. At first not particularly deemed worthy by John Muir as a son-in-law, it seems Buel eventually gained influence in the aging Muir's financial affairs. What about Walter Fiss, who lived in the Bottle House at the ranch? What light might this talented photographer with radical political notions shed on those around him? Or the dozens of others who passed through the ranch and the hundreds through Daggett. The anomalies, and the potential for telling opportunities, go on and on. Northeast of the Van Dyke Ranch a couple of hundred yards is a huge, handsome, red-tiled mansion rising out of a grove of palms, built by Helen and Buel after John Muir's death. The most lavish home for perhaps a hundred miles around, what on earth is it doing there?*

Even Theodore and son Dix have huge gaps in their lives. Especially in rural areas, such prominent figures generate stories, many of them intriguing, that grow and take on their own lives and are finally accepted as fact, though they remain unconfirmed by documentation. The search continues for the complete record of Theodore's divorce and of the lawsuits flying about the ranch. This not out of any particular taste for scandal but because the information in such files might tell a great deal about social dynamics and land development on the Mojave.

Chances are woefully good that such documents are gone forever. Fortunately, however, the people of Daggett care about their sometimes brusque past, and they tend to keep the physical evidence from it. Sometimes late at night, considering the stories, one imagines Daggett, its attics and cellars and sheds overflowing with journals bound in leather, with sheaves of letters tied with string, and shoe boxes stuffed with photographs.

What's to be done in Daggett and elsewhere across the vast Mo-

---

*Apparently, this huge building was one more in a long string of schemes by Buel, something of a happy-go-lucky luftmensch, in the course of using up his wife's inheritance. This dream involved creating a "high-class sanitarium" for tuberculars ("Casa Desierto Sanitarium Will Be Re-opened January"). The building also was called Desertaire. Isolated as it was, and probably undercapitalized to boot, the visionary project, as with others that Buel dreamed up, was all but doomed to failure.

jave? It is unlikely that some wealthy person will sweep into the Mojave. Following the pattern that has given us many of the world's great manuscript collections, such as the Huntington, would he erect a sumptuous repository on a hilltop and send his agents out across the desert to buy up the manuscripts now moldering under the attic eaves of the Mojave's residents? Nor does the government have the will or the sustained resources to accomplish such a task. Assembling the major pieces likely won't involve a project with major funding and teams of historians, anthropologists, and sociologists descending on a town and wringing it dry of information. That likely would be viewed as an assault.

In practical terms, what needs to be done is more of what's already taking place in the towns across the Mojave: the residents further encouraging one another to discover their heritage by gathering what each holds individually. As reflected in the activities of the local historical societies, their spirit is good and their motivation is high, and the hoped-for result will be the enrichment both of their children and of the much wider public interested in the complex relationships of people with each other and their land.

Relating to such issues, a much larger context surrounds both Daggett's history and present efforts to preserve it. To visitors passing through, the Mojave Desert may seem a haughtily placid and grand expanse. In truth it's a place in turmoil. In recent years, the Mojave has become a focus for the old debate about America, one going back to the warring exchanges between John Muir and Gifford Pinchot. Should we preserve our natural heritage or exploit it? Some people argue, rightly, that after a century of activity by miners, cattlemen, and the military, the Mojave hardly is pristine. Then, so the thinking goes, perhaps not so rightly, we might as well follow the precedent of our stalwart ancestors and continue more of the same. Others point out that our forebears may have been stalwart, but times have changed. Today, on a far more crowded planet, destruction of nature hardly is its own excuse for "more of the same." Now we are at a turning point, in the position of a desperate opportunity to turn the old, abusive ways around and save what's left.

Having been in the middle of both sides for years and sympathetic to both, I pretend to no preternatural wisdom on this score. I've known ranchers whose families go back generations on this land. These proud people often would be the first to shore up the slumping foundations of the old ranch house in order to preserve family tradition, yet they would think any restrictions on their activities concerning their larger home, the public lands they use for grazing, as personal assaults to their freedom. All this is further complicated by resentment toward a government seen, again often rightly, as a blind, repressive force. Often the attitude is leavened with the old fantasy that the desert is too vast to be ruined. Yet I've seen, too, that laissez faire does not work on this land, have seen that overgrazing and mining can make a permanent wreck of a beautiful place for all who come after. On the other hand, city people often are offensive in their treatment of locals. They want to drive to the end of a freeway, then, buoyed by their own selfishness, have a wilderness romping ground for their weekend pleasures free of blemishes, those indications of honest people making a living.

Since all of us are creatures of self-interest, masters of rationalizing whatever we find convenient to believe, there is no resolving such positions. Here, the ironies abound. Hailing from some of the most ecologically disturbed places on the planet, urbanites come to the desert wanting to fulfill their Bambi fantasies of nature, while the hardscrabble locals, living in the bosom of nature, simply to survive need to turn every little purchase they have on nature into a dollar. Either way, preservation or exploitation, good people will get hurt. And though on either side individuals wax hot, they may well be missing the greatest irony of all, that forces beyond our control, such as population growth and the food supply, are driving us, not our own bickering on this planet. Still, I can't help feeling, even if the world crisps into a cinder tomorrow, that the angels applaud us not for the fatness of our wallets but for whatever steps we take, whether in our selfish interests or against them, to preserve the richness, both of nature and of history, here on the desert and elsewhere.

Select Bibliography

"Another Corpse Found in the Desert." *Los Angeles Times,* 6 March 1903, 6.

Banham, Peter Reyner. *Scenes in America Deserta.* Salt Lake City: Gibbs M. Smith, 1982.

Banker, Catherine Mary Courser. "A Structural History of the Old Stone Hotel in Daggett Utilizing Archaeological and Documentary Evidence." M.A. thesis, California State University, San Bernardino, 1994.

Beal, Mary. "Lip-Ferns on the Desert." *Desert Magazine* 11.1 (November 1947): 30.

———. "These Plants Sponge Upon Their Neighbors." *Desert Magazine* 10.12 (October 1947): 18.

———. "When John O' Birds Saw Calico." *Calico Print* 7.8 (August 1951): 1, 3.

Carr, Harry C. "Mrs. Wells' Gold Spike Unites Salt Lake Lines." *Los Angeles Times,* 31 January 1905, 1.

———. "Ready-Made Towns Dumped Off Trains." *Los Angeles Times,* 2 February 1905, editorial section, 1, 6.

———. "Wolves on Desert after Greek's Cash." *Los Angeles Times,* 1 February 1905, 1.

"Casa Desierto Sanitarium Will Be Re-opened January." *Barstow Printer Review* [Calif.], 25 December 1924, 1.

Casebier, Dennis G. *The Battle at Camp Cady.* Tales of the Mojave Road 2. Norco: Dennis G. Casebier, 1972.

———. *Carleton's Pah-Ute Campaign.* Tales of the Mojave Road 1. Norco: Dennis G. Casebier, 1972.

———. *Goffs and Its Schoolhouse: The Historic Cultural Center of the East Mojave Desert.* Tales of the Mojave Road 21. Essex: Tales of the Mojave Road Publishing Co., 1995.

Census of 1900, for Los Angeles, Calif. Enumeration District 28: 9.

Census of 1920, for Daggett, Calif. Enumeration District 143: 2.

Chase, J. Smeaton. *Our Araby: Palm Springs and the Garden of the Sun.* Pasadena: Privately printed, 1920.

Crane, Stephen. "The Bride Comes to Yellow Sky." *McClure's Magazine* 10 (February 1898): 377–84.

"Cruel Desert's Victim Said To Be Scott." *Los Angeles Times,* 18 February 1903, 4.

Darlington, David. *The Mojave: A Portrait of the Definitive American Desert.* New York: Henry Holt, 1996.

Divorce Decree of Theodore S. Van Dyke v. Lois A. Van Dyke. Case 32751. Filed 21 April 1899, finalized 5 July 1899. Los Angeles Superior Court, County Records Center Archives. A related action, Case 31251, is missing.

Fletcher, Ed. *Memoirs of Ed Fletcher.* San Diego: Privately printed, 1952.

Jaeger, Edmund C. *The California Deserts.* 1933. Stanford: Stanford University Press, 1965.

Keeling, Patricia Jernigan, ed. *Once upon a Desert: A Bicentennial Project.* 1976. 2d ed. Barstow: Mojave River Valley Museum Association, 1994.

Lane, Lucy Bell. *Calico Memories of Lucy Bell Lane.* Ed. Alan Baltazar. Barstow: Calico Historical Society, 1993.

Lee, W. Storrs. *The Great California Deserts.* New York: Putnam, 1963.

Minneola Valley on the Santa Fe Route. Promotional brochure. Los Angeles: Commercial Printing House, 1894(?).

"M'Kinney Dies Fighting Officers at Bakersfield." *Los Angeles Times,* 20 April 1903, 10.

Moon, Germaine L. Ramounachou. *Barstow Depots and Harvey Houses.* Barstow: Mojave River Valley Museum Association, 1980.

Muir, John. *The Microform Edition of the John Muir Papers, 1858–1957.* Reel 19. Ed. Ronald H. Limbaugh and Kirsten E. Lewis. University of the Pacific, Stockton, Calif., 1986.

———. *Stickeen.* 1909. Berkeley: Heyday Books, 1981.

"Murdered for Money in Lonely Spot." *Los Angeles Times,* 27 February 1903, 6.

Peirson, Erma. *The Mojave River and Its Valley.* Glendale: Arthur H. Clark, 1970.

Renehan, Edward J., Jr. *John Burroughs: An American Naturalist.* Post Mills, Vt.: Chelsea Green, 1992.

Roosevelt, Theodore, et al. *The Deer Family.* New York: Grosset, 1902.

Selvas, Carita. "Life on the Desert." *Desert Magazine* 16.6 (June 1953): 20–21.

Smythe, William E. *History of San Diego, 1542–1908.* 2 vols. San Diego: History, 1908.

Steinbeck, John. *The Grapes of Wrath.* New York: Viking, 1939.

Stone, Joe. "T. S. Van Dyke Paved Way for San Diego Water." *San Diego Union,* 13 August 1973, sec. B, 3.

Van Dyke, Dix [as told to Philip Johnston]. "Law on the Desert." *Westways* 29.11 (November 1937): 14–16.

———. Letter to Alice [Salisbury], 22 December 1949. Mojave River Valley Museum, Barstow, Calif.

———. Manuscript. Untitled and undated onionskin typescript, a variation with some pages missing, of "The Pioneer Story" (see below). Mojave River Valley Museum, Barstow, Calif.

———. "A Modern Interpretation of the Garcés Route." *Annual Publications, Historical Society of Southern California* 13 (1927): 353–59.

———. [as told to Philip Johnston]. "Old Times in Daggett." *Westways* 35.2, pt. 1 (February 1943): 16–17.

———. Personal papers. A miscellany of letters, typescripts, notes, and articles. Contains some rough draft material of "The Pioneer Story" (see below). Feldheym Library, San Bernardino, Calif.

———. Personal papers. A miscellany of letters, typescripts, notes, and articles, many of the latter by Dix's father, Theodore. San Diego Historical Society, San Diego, Calif.

———. "The Pioneer Story." Dix's reminiscences of Daggett published in the *Barstow Printer Review*. They appeared in 1953 under various titles, such as "The Pioneer Story" and "Pioneer Days," on the following Thursdays: 16 April, 23 April, 30 April, 7 May, 28 May, 4 June, 9 July, 16 July, 23 July, 30 July, 6 August, 13 August, 20 August, 27 August, 3 September, 10 September, 17 September, 1 October, 8 October, 15 October, 22 October, 29 October, 5 November, 12 November, 19 November, 3 December, and 10 December.

———. "Recollections of Boyhood Days in San Diego, 1880–1895." Carbon typescript. San Diego Historical Society, 1952.

———. "The Van Dyke Papers: Historic Routes in the Mojave Desert, Compiled from the Notes of Dix Van Dyke." Ed. Wes Chambers. *Quarterly* [of the San Bernardino County Museum Association] 38.1 (Spring 1991): 31–45.

Van Dyke, John C. *The Autobiography of John C. Van Dyke.* Ed. Peter Wild. Salt Lake City: University of Utah Press, 1993.

———. *The Desert: Further Studies in Natural Appearances.* New York: Scribner's, 1901.

———. *The Desert: Further Studies in Natural Appearances.* Photographs by J. Smeaton Chase and notes by Dix Van Dyke. New York: Scribner's, 1930.

————. *The Raritan: Notes on a River and a Family.* New Brunswick, N.J.: Privately printed, 1915.

Van Dyke, Theodore Strong. *County of San Diego: The Italy of Southern California.* San Diego: San Diego Union, 1886.

————. *Flirtation Camp: Or, the Rifle, Rod, and Gun in California.* New York: Fords, Howard, and Hulbert, 1881.

————. "The Forest Primeval: The Opening of the Year." *Outing Magazine* 50.2 (May 1907): 232–35.

————. *Game Birds at Home.* New York: Fords, Howard, and Hulbert, 1895.

————. "In the Big Woods of Oregon: An Impressive Solitude." *Outing Magazine* 47.5 (February 1906): 613–18.

————. *Millionaires of a Day: An Inside History of the Great Southern California "Boom".* New York: Fords, Howard, and Hulbert, 1890.

————. Paintings. Two untitled, undated watercolors, of desert mountains, approximately 12" × 18" and 8" × 14", signed "T. S. Van Dyke." Archives of the Mojave River Valley Museum, Barstow, Calif.

————. *Rifle, Rod, and Gun in California: A Sporting Romance.* New York: Fords, Howard, and Hulbert, 1881. This is a variant title for *Flirtation Camp.*

————. *Southern California: Its Valleys, Hills, and Streams; Its Animals, Birds* . . . New York: Fords, Howard, and Hulbert, 1886.

————. *The Still-Hunter.* New York: Fords, Howard, and Hulbert, 1883.

————. "The Surprising Desert." *Collier's Outdoor America* 46.25 (11 March 1911): 20–21.

Waitman, Leonard. "The History of Camp Cady." *Historical Society of Southern California Quarterly* 36.1 (March 1954): 49–91.

Walker, Clifford J. *Back Door to California: The Story of the Mojave River Trail.* Barstow: Mojave River Valley Museum Association, 1986.

Walker, Franklin. *A Literary History of Southern California.* Berkeley: University of California Press, 1950.

Weight, Harold, and Lucile Weight. Personal papers. Mojave Desert Heritage and Cultural Association, Goffs, Calif.

Weight, Lucile. *The Floral World of Mary Beal.* N.p., 1969. Available through Mitchell Caverns Natural Preserve, Essex, Calif.

Wild, Peter. *Interviews and Notes Regarding John C. Van Dyke.* Archives of the American Academy of Arts and Letters, New York City, and of the University of Arizona, Tucson. Sealed until 2009. Addenda contain photographs and notes from visits to Daggett and the Van Dyke Ranch.

————. "John Muir and the Desert Connection." *John Muir Newsletter* 5.2 (Spring 1995): 2, 6.

————. "John Muir and the Van Dyke Ranch: Intimacy and Desire in His Final Years. Part One." *John Muir Newsletter* 5.3 (Summer 1995): 1, 4–5.

————. "John Muir and the Van Dyke Ranch: Intimacy and Desire in His Final Years. Part Two." *John Muir Newsletter* 5.4 (Fall 1995).

————. "Mary Beal: Pioneer Botanist on the Mojave Desert." *Wildflower* [Canada] 12.5 (Winter 1996): 42–45.

————. *Theodore Strong Van Dyke.* Boise: Boise State University, 1995.

————. "A Writer in a Wild Frontier Town: The Contributions of Theodore Strong Van Dyke." *South Dakota Review* 32.3 (Fall 1994): 51–64.

Wild, Peter, and Neil Carmony. "The Trip Not Taken: John C. Van Dyke, Heroic Doer or Armchair Seer?" *Journal of Arizona History* 34.1 (Spring 1993): 65–80.

[Williams, Robert]. "Daggett Pioneer Cemetery." Typescript of nine pages listing interments with vital statistics. "Compiled by Daggett Pioneer Cemetery Association, Lawrence Alf, Director, March 1990."

Wolfe, Linnie Marsh. *Son of the Wilderness: The Life of John Muir.* New York: Knopf, 1945.

Workman, Boyle. *The City That Grew.* Los Angeles: Southland Publishing, 1935.

Wyatt, David. *The Fall into Eden: Landscape and Imagination in California.* London: Cambridge University Press, 1986.

Index

Peter Wild was born in Northampton, Massachusetts, in 1940. He received B.A. and M.A. degrees in English from the University of Arizona, and completed an M.F.A. in creative writing at the University of California, Irvine. He is one of the foremost poets of the American West, has published dozens of articles in such publications as the *New York Times, Sierra, Smithsonian,* and *Western American Literature,* and is the author and editor of more than forty books, among them *The Desert Reader* (Utah, 1991), *The Saguaro Forest* (Northland, 1986), and *Chihuahua* (Doubleday, 1976). He was nominated for the Pulitzer Prize in 1973 and in 1991 received first prize in poetry from *New Mexico Humanities Review.* Wild has taught at the University of Arizona since 1971, and became full professor of English in 1979.

Library of Congress Cataloging-in-Publication Data

Van Dyke, Dix.
Daggett : life in a Mojave frontier town / Dix Van Dyke ; edited by Peter
Wild.
    p.   cm. — (Creating the North American landscape)
    Includes bibliographical references (p.   ) and index.
    ISBN 0-8018-5625-6 (alk. paper)
    1. Daggett (Calif.) — History.   2. Daggett (Calif.) — Biography.
3. Frontier and pioneer life — California — Daggett.   I. Wild, Peter,
1940-   .   II. Title.   III. Series.
F869.D22V36   1997
979.4'95 — DC21   97-1926
                                                                      CIP